For And

May you live a life

free of cuckoos and

full of purpose!

[signature]

Praise for *The Cuckoo Syndrome*

"Andrea intimately understands the human heart and the heart of God. As a follower of Jesus and with over a decade of clinical experience counseling hurting people, she powerfully integrates Scripture, science, and psychology. Andrea's words, equally elegant and surprisingly provocative, demonstrate that by facing our deepest heartaches and identifying the lies we believe, transformation and healing happen. You will be welcomed into an honest conversation with yourself, God, and others about your wants, needs, and desires. You'll discover what or who is keeping you stuck is not what you think it is. *The Cuckoo Syndrome* is driven by the truth of John 8:32 that the truth will set you free."

—Mark Batterson, lead pastor of National Community Church and *New York Times* best-selling author of nineteen books including *The Circle Maker*, *In a Pit with a Lion on a Snowy Day*, and *Wild Goose Chase*

"Andrea Anderson Polk's *The Cuckoo Syndrome* is a very personal story about overcoming toxic relationships and self-sabotaging behaviors to find the courage to be ourselves. Taking vignettes both from her therapy practice and her own life, Andrea uses the cuckoo bird metaphor to describe both the people in our lives who prey on our vulnerabilities as well as the unconscious ways we can prevent ourselves from acting upon our own best interests. This book is also a very accessible primer on emotion theory, providing the reader with many examples of how accessing core feelings provides a compass for living our lives. To find our true desires and life's purpose, Andrea suggests that we must address the psychological defenses (the various disguises of the cuckoo) that we developed in childhood to protect ourselves from difficult relationships and experiences. These internalized cuckoo tendencies allowed us to survive traumatic and overwhelming experiences but result in a variety of destructive behaviors. Such a journey of the soul can be harrowing, and Andrea suggests that we can find resolve and courage by tapping into the unconditional love of past caregivers and by developing an open and deeply personal relationship with Christ."

—Stuart Andrews, Ph.D., Faculty Chair, The Intensive Short-term Dynamic Psychotherapy Program at the Washington School of Psychiatry, and coauthor of *Treating Affect Phobia: A Manual for Short-Term Dynamic Psychotherapy*

"One of the true blessings I have experienced as a professor is to see students grow and thrive in their calling. Through hard work and personal struggle, Andrea stands out among her peers as a gifted professional counselor, speaker, and writer. Andrea writes with compassion, empathy, and transparency. *The Cuckoo Syndrome* will help readers overcome false thinking and enable them to learn how to challenge their thinking, listen to their hearts, and trust their emotions to live fully and joyfully in the present."

—Kathleen Arveson, Ph.D., Senior Lecturer, Department of Psychology and Counseling, Regent University

THE
CUCKOO
SYNDROME

THE SECRET TO BREAKING FREE FROM UNHEALTHY RELATIONSHIPS, TOXIC THINKING, AND SELF-SABOTAGING BEHAVIOR

ANDREA ANDERSON POLK
LICENSED PROFESSIONAL COUNSELOR

Forefront
BOOKS

To My Mother
My eternal gratitude to you for taking a courageous
stand for truth and paving our way to freedom.

CONTENTS

AUTHOR'S NOTE

MY THERAPEUTIC WORK AS A LICENSED PROFESSIONAL counselor has inspired this book. I have spoken to and counseled hundreds, possibly thousands of people about the subjects covered inside, all of whom have motivated me on this journey.

The Cuckoo Syndrome is a compilation of my story, the clinical experience gained from more than a decade of close attention and treatment of my clients in private practice, and the study of psychological research. All of which I have developed into an innovative strategy for breaking free from unhealthy relationships, toxic thinking, and self-sabotaging behavior (i.e., cuckoos). Consequently, this creates space for one's purpose to "hatch" and come to life and no longer be destroyed and suffocated by the cuckoo.

As a clinician, I strongly believe we can only take our clients as far as we are willing to go ourselves.

At the prompting and encouragement of my clients to write a book, I feel honored to present my work to you in this volume.

ARE CUCKOOS REAL BIRDS?

Sitting in your office was a healing balm for my soul. It was the first time I had ever had the courage to confront the truth that I was in an emotionally and spiritually abusive marriage. This healing journey to freedom released me from my prison. I no longer feel lost. I was stuck and suffering silently far too long. I have courageously and victoriously taken back my life.

THIS CLIENT, LIKE SO MANY OTHERS, HAD SAT UNDER MY counsel after seeing a number of professional therapists, pastors, mentors, lay ministers, and others who were all trying to fix her and her abusive marriage, yet she felt crazier and crazier. It was not until she realized she was sitting under the toxic weight of a cuckoo relationship that she was able to begin the process of freedom.

Did you know a cuckoo is a *real* bird?

Imagine it is a beautiful spring day, and you are sitting in your favorite spot at home and relaxing, and you notice a robin in her nest outside your window.

You also notice a large, ugly bird, a cuckoo bird, watching the robin's nest from a nearby tree. As soon as the mother robin leaves her nest, the cuckoo bird swoops in, removes a robin's egg, and while holding it in her beak, lays her own egg directly in the robin's nest along with the robin's other eggs. The cuckoo bird then flies off, devouring the robin's egg as she makes her getaway!

In taking a closer look at the robin's nest you are shocked at what you see. The cuckoo's egg looks eerily similar and almost identical to the robin's eggs; it is a light shade of blue with small brown speckles. The resemblance is uncanny! You are curious to watch and see what the mother robin will do when she returns to her nest to incubate her eggs. Surely, she would notice this foreign egg in her nest, even though it looks like one of her own. But once she returns, she sits on the cuckoo bird's egg and treats it as if it were her own. She's been tricked. In fact, she continues to sit on her eggs day after day and eventually one hatches. It is the cuckoo chick and only the cuckoo chick. The robin's other eggs have not yet hatched.

Almost immediately upon hatching, the featherless cuckoo chick, with its eyes still closed, uses its wings to push some of the robin's eggs out of the nest. It's almost as if it was born with innate knowledge to kill the other eggs in the nest. The robin returns with a worm to feed the cuckoo chick because she believes it is her young. Day after day you witness the mother and father robins exhausting themselves to feed the cuckoo chick, which has an insatiable appetite. It never seems to be satisfied as the cuckoo chick is constantly calling out for food and attention. Your heart breaks as you look on in shock at the robins who are feeding this thing that does not even belong to them, yet they believe it is their young! The cuckoo chick grows larger and larger, very quickly outgrowing the robin parents. Any remaining robin eggs are ejected or smothered by the cuckoo chick. Even after the cuckoo chick grows and exits the nest, the robins continue to feed it and follow its distinctive call, *cuckoo ... cuckoo ...*, leaving the robins drained and depleted as empty nesters with no robin chicks of their own.

If your curiosity has gotten the best of you and you want a visual of the cuckoo bird, you'll see a picture at the very beginning of chapter 1.

As a counselor who spent years studying the human condition, I couldn't help but wonder: can our most intimate relationships and our own self-sabotaging behaviors resemble that of a cuckoo—nature's infamous imposter?

I have listened to thousands of stories, worked with thousands of individuals and couples, and followed my own curiosity about the cuckoo as patterns and common experiences began to emerge. The cuckoo bird represents unhealthy relationships, toxic thinking, and self-sabotaging behaviors that secretly creep into our lives when we least expect them. I've used the cuckoo analogy and illustration in my counseling practice with nearly all my clients at some point during their treatment.

Cuckoos are invisible enemies that deceptively and elusively consume your time, energy, and attention. Ultimately cuckoos hijack your life, and you find yourself left with a haunting confusion and chronic emptiness as you wander through your days feeling lost, with no purpose of your own. This invisible enemy is hidden only to be revealed when it feels like it is too late or the suffering is too great.

I came to the cuckoo metaphor through my own story. My journey of healing coincided with my parents' divorce and a particularly difficult season of my life. That was decades ago, and since that time, I have spent my career as a licensed professional counselor and supervisor treating relationship issues. Numerous clients have come to me feeling overwhelmed, stuck, and powerless. I have studied both the research and my clients, and I have concluded that we all experience the Cuckoo Syndrome.

Do you have a cuckoo in your life, your nest, right now and you don't even recognize it? Are you the one doing all the work in the relationship? Have you succumbed to an ever-demanding, never-satisfied person who leaves you feeling as if you are not enough?

Throughout this book, my story is interwoven with the stories of my clients to create clarity and direction for those who have reached an impasse, suffering in the turmoil that shadows a destructive relationship. It is through the combination of my own lived experience, the close attention given to my clients, and the study of psychological and spiritual research that I have developed this practical guide to breaking free from the cuckoo's snare.

The Cuckoo Syndrome gives you a long-term successful strategy to fend off these cuckoos that invade your life so you are not prone and susceptible to being a target for future cuckoos.

Each chapter addresses the cuckoo's various disguises. There is the cuckoo of not feeling your feelings, the cuckoo of unresolved grief, the fear cuckoo, the shame cuckoo, the stress cuckoo, the perfectionism cuckoo, you as the cuckoo, the abuse cuckoo, the counselor cuckoo, and probably the most insidious cuckoo of all, the religion cuckoo.

If your cuckoo is the culprit, then discovering your purpose is the antidote to the cuckoo. The final chapters of this book answer the question, "Now that I learned how to identify my cuckoo, what now?"

Your attention will shift from the cuckoo in your life to pursuing your passions and embracing your heart's deepest desires. You will begin to identify your purpose beyond your cuckoos and the suffering they inflict and take back what has been stolen from your nest that has never been allowed to hatch.

CHAPTER 1

THE CUCKOO IN YOUR NEST

Do Your Relationships Resemble Cuckoos?

Insanity is doing the same thing over and over again and expecting different results.
—ALBERT EINSTEIN

MY FATHER SAT CROSS-LEGGED ON MY PARENTS' BED WITH A loaded gun in his lap and threatened to kill himself if my mother left him.

Decades later, as a professional counselor who has spent years studying the human condition, I recognized the Cuckoo Syndrome, a group of symptoms that collectively indicate a predictable yet invisible pattern of unhealthy relationships, toxic thinking, and self-sabotaging behavior that lead to unnecessary suffering. At its core the Cuckoo Syndrome is an imposter that seeks to mimic who you are and what you want.

The Cuckoo Syndrome is a nonscientific and nonclinical term that allows complicated, psychological concepts such as personality disorders, mental illness, codependency, trauma, attachment styles, emotional and spiritual abuse, and addictions to become easier to understand and relate to. I've discovered in my treatment of thousands of clients that most people do not know exactly what these terms mean, how they show up practically in our everyday lives, and how to translate them into our lives.

The Cuckoo Syndrome can deceitfully and subtly erode our careers, our ministries, and our most intimate relationships, including the relationships we have with ourselves. In this way, the Cuckoo Syndrome shows up as a chronic neglect of self due to consistently taking care of someone else, receiving little or no reciprocation, or unknowingly living a counterfeit purpose. Ultimately you find yourself lost, wandering through life with haunting confusion, lingering emptiness, and persistent grief.

Let's begin by understanding the biological nature of the cuckoo bird. Researchers who have studied cuckoos for hundreds of years have found a vicious, shocking, secret life of these predatory creatures in their natural habitats.

The Predatory, Secretive Life of the Cuckoo Bird Exposed

This cuckoo bird is a brood parasite. "Brood parasites use various gimmicks to deceive the hosts into slaving for them."[1] A parasite is someone or something who lives and feeds on another person or thing and causes harm to its host. Parasites "habitually take advantage of the generosity of others without making any useful return."[2] Does this dynamic feel familiar to any of your relationships?

> Of all the birds in the world, none may be as clever and cruel as brood parasites. These opportunistic animals dump their eggs into another species' nest to avoid wasting time and energy on childcare. Their life strategy is built upon tricking other birds, so perhaps they've learned the nasty reputation that precedes them.[3]

Similarly, human cuckoos are opportunistic and aim to take advantage of you and monopolize your time and energy by dumping their issues into your life. Persons living with a cuckoo in their nest are often initially unaware they are habitually taking care of this person even though this invisible, injurious behavior is right in front of them. They are aware, however, that something feels off, something doesn't feel OK, and something is missing, yet they can't put their finger on how or why.

A fascinating genetic fact about female parasitic cuckoo birds is that they "have secretive and fast-laying behaviors"[4] as well as an ability to lay cryptic eggs or "eggs that closely resemble the eggs of their chosen host"[5] to a shocking extent:

> The parasite's eggs have a number of tricks up their shells, too. They often mimic host eggs in color and shape—so the nest owners don't notice the eggs aren't theirs—and also

have thicker shells and shorter incubation times, which
allow the invading offspring to hatch first.[6]

The cuckoo bird's eggs can look nearly identical to the host eggs!
The host parents have been tricked. Similarly, human cuckoos mimic
the behaviors and desires of other people to trick them into letting
them into their life and forming relationships with them. Human
cuckoos adopt a devious disguise. As they get to know another
person, they seek to prey on their weaknesses and vulnerabilities
in order to use them and take advantage of their kindness and their
deeper need to be known, to be loved, and to have companionship,
which every human being requires.

Chances are if the Cuckoo Syndrome is manifesting in one of
your relationships, it will infect seemingly unrelated areas of your
life as well. Cuckoos create cuckoos; they multiply by passing off
their eggs to the nests of the other birds they invade and destroy
the eggs that are already present:

If the parasite makes it out of its egg (cue the *Jaws* theme),
then it's often time for a real massacre . . . a newborn
Common Cuckoo wiggles its way around the Reed
Warbler's nest, using its shoulders and back to push out
all three of the host's eggs. Brood parasites, it seems, are
basically born evil . . . while still blind and featherless, will
stab the host's chicks to death with its hooked beak.[7]

Human cuckoo relationships not only invade your life, but
they also want to toss your purpose, hopes, and dreams, your
so-called eggs, right out of your life and replace them so you will
nurture and take care of theirs instead of your own.

Are you thinking of a certain relationship right now that creates
a similar cycle of suffering in your life? Do you feel like a slave to

someone else's needs, nurturing their dreams at the expense of your own?

Now that the cuckoo chick has hatched, the host parents become extremely exhausted keeping up with this ever-demanding, never-satisfied cuckoo chick that is always needing them.

Image Credit: Bill Kersey

"Little warbler feeding a cuckoo chick and seeming to risk being devoured itself as it bows deep into the enormous gape to feed a very young bird many times its own size."[8]

This is just the beginning. It's a long, hard life.

As you can see from the image, a cuckoo chick egg hatches first and grows extremely large very quickly, even bigger than the host parents!

Take a moment as you look at this image. Imagine who the cuckoo is in your nest. Does it evoke a tinge of sadness as you look at the host parent feeding the cuckoo chick? Perhaps even anger? How do you feel toward the cuckoo in your nest?

The cuckoo chick's insatiable appetite consumes all the attention, time, and energy of the host parents who must feed it constantly. This is because "the young cuckoo needs as much food as four young reed warblers."[9] The host parents continue feeding and caring for the cuckoo chick, working to meet its every need, and it is not even their young. The host parents are deceived into believing the cuckoo chick is their own and they exhaust themselves while taking care of it.

The cuckoo chick will destroy the remaining host eggs, if it hasn't killed them already, due to its huge size, eventually crushing them. The cuckoo chick not only becomes the host parents' entire life's purpose, but they also have no chicks, no purpose of their own.

Sadly, the host eggs never hatch and come to life.

Cuckoos are, in essence, nature's brilliant, masterful manipulators.

Can you relate to the host parent? Perhaps like the host eggs, your own purposes (hopes, dreams, desires) never came to life. They are smothered by the cuckoo in your life. Who has your eggs? Your energy, time, and care are given away to nurturing an unhealthy relationship that is now bringing you hurt and harm.

Do Your Relationships Resemble a Cuckoo, Nature's Infamous Deceiver and Taker?

There are two ways the Cuckoo Syndrome can show up:

1. The Relationship Cuckoo: Unhealthy, dysfunctional, and lopsided relationships

2. The Self-Inflicted Cuckoo: Toxic thinking patterns and self-sabotaging behavior

The Relationship Cuckoo

Now that you have been considering whether or not you have a cuckoo in your nest, here are some questions to help you identify if you are hosting the relationship cuckoo:

1. Is there someone in your life who tries to monopolize your time and consumes a lot of your energy?
2. Is there someone in your life who is more of a taker than a giver and does not give back to you in the same way?
3. Is there someone in your life who leaves you feeling overwhelmed because your purpose in life revolves around them, and your voice, feelings, and needs are not mutually acknowledged?
4. Is there someone in your life with whom you are unable to have a rational conversation because simple things become very complicated?
5. Is there someone in your life who leaves you feeling confused and misunderstood, but you cannot put your finger on exactly how or why?
6. Is there someone in your life who you feel manipulates you, and your gut is telling you something is not right?
7. Is there someone in your life for whom you feel responsible carrying the emotional weight of the relationship?
8. Is there someone in your life you feel has been gradually deceiving you over a period of time, and you realize this person is not who you thought they were?
9. Is there someone in your life who is never satisfied, no matter how much you try to love, help, and please them?

10. Is there someone in your life who twists the truth and avoids dealing with facts and becomes accusatory, critical, or overly emotional when you try to point it out?

If you can relate to any of these questions, who is the person with whom you are in a cuckoo relationship? Name them here:

_____

_____

_____

If you answered *no* to all of the questions, your cuckoo might not be a relationship. Instead, you might have a self-inflicted cuckoo: toxic thinking or a self-sabotaging behavior, which will be addressed in the next section. Alternatively, perhaps you realize you are displaying some cuckoo-type behavior in your relationships.

The Cuckoo Syndrome can show up in unhealthy relationships with a friend, spouse, mentor, pastor, counselor, sibling, parent, colleague, boss, or significant other.

It can also be a role you adopt based on a situation or event where you have taken on more responsibility than you are capable of handling—roles that allow you to feel needed and loved such as caretaker, the always-on-call person, the fixer, the peacemaker, or the rescuer. The Cuckoo Syndrome can sound like this: "I'm always the person who . . ." For example, maybe you are the one who always organizes the carpool or schedules all the Zoom calls or does all the household chores or pays the bills or runs all the errands. Perhaps your spouse suffers from a chronic illness and you are going beyond your capacity to take care of him or her because you believe your needs are not as important as theirs since you are not the one who is sick. You have falsely believed it is your sole responsibility to carry the full load. Deep down you feel resentful and have a strong desire to be alone and numb out.

Our choices and associated behaviors offer some form of benefit or we would not be operating in a situation where we are absorbing the responsibility for another person or group of people. If you are the pleaser, caretaker, peacemaker, rescuer, or fixer, ask yourself, *What am I getting from this role?* Perhaps you feel worthy, important, or needed. Ask yourself, *What does this role allow me to avoid?* Perhaps you avoid painful emotions such as the guilt from saying *no* and not being there for someone, or you avoid the fear of disappointing people you care about, or you are avoiding your own difficult issues.

Here is an example.

It's the holiday season. You discuss with your spouse and make the decision that for Christmas this year you are going to vacation alone with your children to enjoy a relaxing change of pace. You want to spend some much-needed fun time together as a family. You want to take a much-needed break from the hustle and bustle to sit on a beach instead of sweating over a hot stove only to engage in the same religious and political conversations year after year.

You finally muster up the courage to tell your extended family you will not be hosting Christmas this year. They respond by trying to guilt-trip you into changing your mind. They are shocked and appalled at your decision.

"How can you break this precious family tradition? After all, you have the nice house and space for everyone, and you are centrally located, so it makes it so much easier on everyone." Your family goes on and on about how their lives are more stressful than yours, how they really need a break. "Why can't you go on vacation this summer instead of taking time off over the holidays?"

After engaging with them and trying to maintain your boundaries and state your needs, you feel the emotional weight of responsibility to make everyone happy. So you tell your spouse, "Let's just host one more year."

These decisions seem miniscule at first, but when the pattern continues in your relationships (chronic caretaking, putting other people's needs above your own, having no boundaries), you eventually find yourself depleted and joyless and your sense of self slowly eroded.

Every relationship requires effort, time, energy, and attention, which in turn require fruits of the Spirit such as love, joy, peace, patience, kindness, goodness, faithfulness, gentleness, and self-control, characteristics found in a healthy relationship. What is most important is that the relationship is mutual because both people are equally attentive to each other's needs, and they sacrifice and compromise accordingly. The problem with a cuckoo relationship is that you deceive yourself into thinking you must do all the work to keep the relationship going, and you continue to nurture, take care of, and feed your cuckoo, and that becomes your primary responsibility.

The most important thing to remember about the cuckoo is that they are imposters packaged in a seemingly good and healthy relationship, disguising themselves as the real thing, and mimicking who they think you want them to be. The issue arises when the other person in the relationship, like the cuckoo bird, perpetually uses you, takes advantage of your kindness and openness, and does not reciprocate. Through a deceptive process, you have falsely come to believe you are being empathetic, patient, forgiving, and kind, when the truth is that you are not long-suffering. You *are* suffering.

Cuckoo Communication

Trying to communicate with the person in your cuckoo relationship about how you feel and what is happening can lead to chronic experiences of feeling disillusioned. They repeatedly make excuses for their hurtful behavior and blame you instead. Many clients say to me, "Maybe it is my fault."

Cuckoo communication tactics are manipulative and deceptive. I explain to my clients, "They complicate the simple and emote the factual." By this, I mean that they twist the truth and avoid dealing with facts/reality in conversation and become overly emotional. They avoid facing the true situation that happened— the real event or situation that was painful or harmful to you. It is difficult to have a rational conversation because they make simple things (the facts) extremely confusing and complicated, leaving you questioning yourself, doubting reality, and wondering if you are somehow wrong.

For example, let's say you are at a company dinner or happy hour for your spouse or significant other when you witness them acting in an inappropriate, romantic way with their colleague. When you gently bring your concern to their attention, they angrily respond, "You're controlling. You want to dictate what I do and who I am friends with. You are just jealous and insecure." Clearly, they are ignoring the reality of what happened between them and their colleague while becoming overly emotional. They are also complicating the facts of what you saw by accusing you of things that are not true.

When conflicts arise, these people are focused on being right instead of being open and desiring to understand your perspective. During conversations, they operate with a closed mentality, expect you to read their mind, and criticize you for not understanding them. If you disagree with them and share your opinion, they take it personally and become offended.

When you share your thoughts and needs, you receive no acknowledgment, and they continue their selfish and harmful behavior patterns toward you. When you share with them how you are feeling, they respond by saying how they feel based on what you said rather than acknowledging your emotions and actively listening to you.

Here are some examples from my counseling sessions:

"When I gently share with my mother that she hurt my feelings, she does not acknowledge me. She changes the subject. It's as if the conversation never happened."

"When I share how I am hurt by something my colleague said or did, I walk away from the conversation feeling confused, as if I have done something wrong."

"When I share my feelings with my friend, he gets defensive, and I end up questioning myself and doubting my own feelings after a conversation with him."

"When sharing my feelings with my father, it never feels like a two-way dialogue. My feelings are dismissed, criticized, or ignored."

"When I tell my sister what I feel, she tells me I shouldn't feel that way. Are my feelings wrong?"

"When I share how I feel with my boyfriend, he seems to have a way of always switching the focus back to himself."

"When I share how I feel with my wife, she responds, 'After all I've done for you, you still don't appreciate me.' I was simply trying to say that my feelings were hurt. And now I seem to have hurt her."

The intent of cuckoo communication is that the person seeks to convince you that you are the dysfunctional and unhealthy one. Like the cuckoo bird, they desire more and more of your time, energy, and attention. The longer you stay in the relationship, feeding their ever-hungry, never-satisfied ego, the larger and larger their feelings become, and your feelings are consumed by theirs. You are filling a void in their life that you were never meant to fill. Meanwhile, your needs, dreams, desires, and purpose never hatch or come to fruition.

The Abusive Relationship Cuckoo: Death by a Thousand Cuts

The Cuckoo Syndrome exists on a spectrum, with some forms of cuckoo-type relationships more damaging and severe than others, such as abuse. Being in a relationship where abuse is present establishes a similar dynamic to that of the cuckoo bird. It feels like death by a thousand cuts, namely, painful moments that take pieces of your soul and bring that pain into your life again and again.

Biologists describe cuckoo birds as "masters of disguise" and "notorious cheats" who prey on an "unsuspecting host" and mirror them to a "startling degree."[10] These parasitic birds are experts at escaping responsibility and intuitively adopt methods of trickery. The abusive process in human relationships is eerily similar and leaves you with a haunting confusion and immense suffering as they invade your life. You are the unsuspecting host they watch carefully, study intuitively, and then prey on. They aim to deceive you by disguising their true self in order to use and take advantage of you. They secretly plan their agenda to harm you and monopolize your time and energy.

An abusive relationship is characterized by a person's demonstrating deception, manipulation, and control, where the other person intentionally harms another person. Abuse comes in many forms, such as physical, verbal, emotional, sexual, and spiritual. Abuse can produce a painful, crazy-making feeling in which the person being abused falsely believes they are overreacting, selfish, difficult to be with, too sensitive, ungrateful, and a failure at relationships. When these lies are repeated often by the abuser, the victim eventually comes to believe them.

Like the cuckoo bird, people who abuse others can be masters of adopting various disguises to hide their true nature and lure their hosts into developing a relationship with them. They are highly intelligent, seeking to exploit weaknesses and vulnerabilities. In the beginning of the relationship, the abusive person can be especially kind and charming, but their deceptive nature slowly turns their kindness and eagerness into manipulation and control.

It might feel good at first to feel important and special: someone pursues you, shows such a strong interest in you and your life, and desires so much of your time. But after a while you start to feel used, lied to, and taken advantage of. Ultimately the relationship revolves around them, and they want you all to themselves.

The relationship is not mutual and reciprocal; it is lopsided and draining. You are the one doing all the work to please them and make them happy, yet they are consistently unsatisfied, and you are wounded in the process. Deep down you believe the lie that you are too much or not enough.

The cuckoo's reactions become intense if you try to set boundaries, have a voice, express your needs, and make room for yourself in the relationship. They can shift blame, accuse, and criticize. Over time you feel severely confused and hurt and are increasingly isolated; your reality becomes altered.

One of the reasons people feel such self-doubt when they are in an abusive relationship is because an abusive person does not manifest abusive tendencies all the time. They can go for long periods without manifesting any abusive behaviors toward you. That is mostly due to the fact that they want to keep you engaged in the relationship. At times they make you feel better than anyone else, and at other times they make you feel lower than anyone else. It is when they feel triggered by you pushing one of their hidden buttons that you are blindsided and shocked by their toxic behavior when it comes to the surface again. They can tend to quietly keep a record of your wrongs and wait for the opportune moment to punish you. As I said, the abuse feels like death by a thousand cuts, painful moments that take pieces of your soul and bring that pain into your life again and again.

A Story of Abuse

Thomas was given a drum set as a Christmas gift from his close friend Dave, who knew Thomas had played in college and hoped to encourage him to pursue his long-lost musical talent that work pressures had displaced. Thomas also enjoyed spending time with his family when he was not working. Dave admired how Thomas prioritized his wife and family; they were his pride and joy. Dave knew Thomas tends to put the needs of others above his own and that he was too busy with work to purchase the drums himself. Upon receiving the drums, Thomas was hesitant and a bit anxious to tell his wife that he was going to take lessons at the local community center after seeing the class advertised in the newspaper.

Once he mustered up the courage to tell her, he left the conversation feeling afraid and guilty for pursuing something he was passionate about outside of his work and family. Thomas's wife criticized him repeatedly: "You are a terrible father for choosing to take lessons for your silly drums over spending time with your own children." "You are going to damage your children because you are going to make them feel abandoned each time you go to your lesson." "You don't really want to spend time with our children or you wouldn't play the drums." "You are trying to avoid the responsibility of being a parent." "I am like a single parent in this family, and you are like another child: selfish and irresponsible."

Rather than celebrate his opportunity to pursue a personal passion and encourage him, despite his fears, she became passive aggressive and did not speak to Thomas. She slept in another room and avoided him for long periods.

Although Thomas pursued his drum lessons, she repeatedly told him he was neglecting his children and her when he played the drums. He began seeking counseling because he felt disoriented and recognized that this painful pattern of constant criticism of him as a father and husband had manifested in other ways for a long time in his marriage. The verbal and emotional abuse had been invisible to him.

The Cuckoo Syndrome slowly erodes your sense of self and thwarts your purpose. As a counselor, I have worked with many individuals and couples where abuse is present in the relationship. At times, abusers are unlikely to seek counseling because they may not want to believe that anything is wrong with them. If they do seek counseling, following through with counseling is also difficult for these individuals because they can become defensive and question the counsel they are given by therapists, who want to help. I have found that these individuals become extremely upset and disappointed when they are not given the answers or the solutions they are seeking or the special treatment they deeply believe they deserve. For this reason, it has been my experience that they tend to jump from counselor to counselor, hoping the next advice from a counselor will align with their behavior.

Based on my experience, when they do seek counseling, it is more often for other symptoms such as substance abuse, infidelity, a work crisis, depression, or anxiety. The problem occurs in the relationship when the person is unwilling to be accountable for their abusive behavior and do the necessary work to change their actions. I have discovered the cuckoo bird analogy serves to reveal what's really going on to the partner in the abusive relationship as they begin to acknowledge the deceit, manipulation, and control and put a name to their pain for the first time.

To repair such a relationship, it is essential that a person in an abusive relationship breaks the silence of their suffering and seeks help. It is necessary for the abusive person to be equally willing to pursue help and do the work necessary to overcome their toxic behavior patterns so they do not continue to hurt their spouse or friend. Chapter 9, "Cuckoo Counsel," will provide some practical steps on when and how to pursue professional counseling, what makes a therapist safe, and what to expect in counseling.

Hurting People Hurt People

Although signs and symptoms resemble other personality disorders or traits, the Cuckoo Syndrome is not a disorder or a pathology. The Cuckoo Syndrome is not about blaming the cuckoo. It is important to note that any of us can behave like a cuckoo or fall into the Cuckoo Syndrome. I've discovered in my treatment of clients over the years that hurting people hurt people.

All people carry their own wounds, unresolved pain, and heartaches from their past. I have worked with numerous individuals who experience intense guilt and regret regarding their abusive behavior and desire to make amends. I have such empathy and compassion for these men and women since there exists an underlying shame, which is primary to why they become defensive and angry and go on the attack quite easily due to their woundedness and delicate ego. I have found that beneath that external facade of self-confidence is a deeper layer of fragility, insecurity, and a fear of being seen as weak and a failure.

I've found they are typically victims of abuse and trauma earlier in life. They can often appear to be arrogant and emotionally distant or cold. This can be a survival mode to compensate for the lack of self due to believing at their core that they are unlovable and unworthy.

The good news is that you can heal regardless of whether or not the cuckoo in your life is willing to do the necessary work to change their unhealthy behavior. They are not responsible for your healing—you are. And with God's help and the help of others, you can be free. Freedom is knowing this truth, which begins to shift how you operate within certain relationships.

It takes courage and deep commitment to do the healing work and not blame other people but still recognize your role in the cuckoo relational dynamic. Acknowledging this truth can be extremely difficult because when we face reality, we face the lies we have been telling ourselves, we face painful emotions that we have buried, and we become aware of just how much our false beliefs and toxic thoughts are contributing to our suffering. Healing consists of knowing the cuckoo relationships we have allowed in our life and the ways we have nurtured them and neglected ourselves in the process.

What Do All Cuckoos Have in Common? They Need a Host. You Are Their Host.

Once you realize the cuckoo-host struggle you are currently experiencing in your relationships, it is important to identify what made your life susceptible to cuckoos in the first place.

If you find yourself continually attracting destructive or lopsided relationships, it is most likely because in some capacity, you were willing to give up your needs, your wants, your thoughts, your feelings, your voice, your boundaries, your hopes, and your dreams. Therefore, you are enabling the Cuckoo Syndrome to be present within your relationships. Additionally, something is missing inside of you that you are hoping the relationship will heal or fix. Or perhaps you have a deep-seated fear of rejection, abandonment, or disappointing others or your identity is found in the need to be needed and as a result, you lose connection to knowing your own needs. Have compassion on yourself and do not shame yourself either. We all have a deep need to be loved and cared for. We all have seasons of life where we are involved in cuckoo-type relationships.

The Cuckoo Syndrome shows up as a chronic neglect of self by consistently taking care of someone you have allowed into your life while receiving little or no reciprocation. Understanding and becoming aware of being the host and how you participate in the cuckoo relationship is essential to the healing process and to reclaiming your life and the eggs in your life that have never been able to hatch.

You are the one who must stop hosting your cuckoo and believing the lie that you are responsible for carrying the emotional weight of the relationship. Other people do not have the power to control you. They can attempt to control you or try to make you feel a certain way or act a certain way, but only if you allow them.

As stated, the Cuckoo Syndrome is not about placing blame on the other person (significant other, family members, ministry leaders, colleagues). The cuckoo is not the problem; the problem is the unhealthy relational dynamic that is occurring between the two of you. You need to acknowledge the role you play in allowing them to become your primary purpose rather than having your own purpose and heart's desires to delight in.

Remember, because cuckoos come into your life disguised as a seemingly good relationship or healthy person, initially you don't know if you have a cuckoo relationship, but you do know something seems off even though you can't quite put your finger on it. You are stuck, exhausted, and have lost precious pieces of yourself.

In the next chapter, "Stuck in Cuckoo Land: How to Deal with the Cuckoos in Your Life" you will learn the tools that will help you to get unstuck and begin the process of finding yourself again.

Start by asking yourself, *Do I make a good host for a cuckoo? "Have I allowed a cuckoo to invade my life? Am I now sitting on their eggs instead of nurturing my own? Am I now exhausting myself feeding and taking care of them?*

The Self-Inflicted Cuckoo

The cuckoo in your life does not have to be an unhealthy relationship with another person; it can be the unhealthy relationship you have within yourself. A self-inflicted cuckoo shows up as an internal battle rather than an external relationship. So instead of a person who continues to hurt you, use you, or take advantage of you, the self-inflicted cuckoo is your own behaviors and thinking patterns that are keeping you stuck.

You might not realize that the things that are holding you back or getting in your way are actually because of your own thinking, actions, and behaviors. We have all been here. Understanding this cuckoo dynamic can help prevent you from shaming yourself when you repeat these destructive behaviors over and over again.

Self-Inflicted Cuckoo = Toxic Thinking Patterns + Self-Sabotaging Behaviors

In my work with thousands of clients, I've discovered that although self-sabotage is a very common experience, most people do not know they are engaging in self-sabotaging behaviors. It is important to note that the words *self-sabotaging* and *self-inflicted* are not designed to shame you or place blame. The purpose is to put a name to specific ways we unknowingly harm ourselves

THE CUCKOO IN YOUR NEST

that leads to unnecessary suffering. What we can name we can heal. Naming this invisible enemy brings truth, not shame, and knowing the truth leads to freedom.

The following questions will you identify if you are hosting the self-inflicted cuckoo:

1. Is there an area of your life that began as a passion and has increasingly grown into an obsessive preoccupation, crippling perfectionism, or worse, an addiction? (For example, your to-do list, social media, work, volunteering, exercise, cleaning, online dating, shopping.)

2. Is there an area of your life where you are feeding your ego because you are more concerned with success, keeping up appearances, and being the best? Do you feel bound to these internal drives that grow bigger and bigger the more you nurture them?

3. Is there an area of your life that initially appeared to be a good thing or a God thing, yet it has left you feeling empty, lost, and lonely? (For example, a ministry, career, project.)

4. Is there an area of your work, home, or social life that has gradually consumed you and become the primary source of your identity, worth, and value?

5. Is there an area of your life where you tend to neglect your mental health and emotional well-being and you experience stress and burnout as a result? Do you also tend to neglect or not prioritize relationships with the people closest to you? (For example, your marriage, friendships, family.)

6. Is there an area of your life that has overtaken you, and the more you try to control it, the more out of control you feel? (For example, food, drugs, work, TV, drinking.)

7. Is there an area of your life in which you have become driven by your performance instead of guided by your

purpose, and where you have lost your peace of mind and joy as a result?

8. Is there an area of your life that originally fulfilled you but now drains you and no longer truly satisfies the longings of your soul or your heart's deepest desires?

Self-inflicted cuckoos appear good on the outside, but they create harm because you gradually develop an obsessive preoccupation that takes over your life. Self-inflicted cuckoos are imposters disguised as things that will fulfill you, yet ultimately they leave you feeling empty, lost, and lonely.

Unlike relationship cuckoos, with self-inflicted cuckoos, you are not feeding the insatiable appetite of an unhealthy person; you are feeding the insatiable appetite of your ego by searching for relief and significance in unhealthy ways.

Self-inflicted cuckoos come in many forms. They can be regular things that become all-consuming and spiral out of control or they can be passions that become obsessions or worse—addictions. Examples of these regular things are your to-do list, online dating, cooking, cleaning, exercising, social media, television, sex, work, food, alcohol, shopping, volunteering, and decorating. None of these things is harmful, wrong, or bad in and of itself.

The danger comes when they slowly consume your daily life and control you rather than you exhibiting self-control over them and using them in moderation. For example, perhaps you turn to your phone to distract yourself from difficult issues and it becomes obsessive; you can't enjoy a moment without it because you are constantly checking Instagram, email, text messages, news, Facebook, and the number of views for your most recent comment, or a YouTube video, or the number of followers and "Likes" you have.

Addictive behaviors—such as alcoholism, disordered eating, sex and love addiction, drug addiction, and workaholism—are also self-inflicted cuckoos. Like the host parent of the cuckoo chick who becomes a slave to its ever-demanding, never-satisfied demands. So it is with self-inflicted cuckoos because you are a servant to your own internal drives that grow bigger and bigger.

Self-inflicted cuckoos can also be an area of your life that begin as a passion and then slowly grow into an obsession and a crippling perfectionism, which can become the sole source of your identity, worth, and value. As a result, you easily feel envious, resentful, competitive, and prideful or push yourself too hard and endure dangerous levels of stress. Examples include being passionate about a project, a ministry, or a career.

The cuckoo arises when your life becomes out of balance and your relationships, mental health, and physical health are affected. Your marriage suffers, you do not spend as much time with your children, you experience chronic fatigue or other unexplained medical symptoms, you are not sleeping well, you struggle with bouts of depression, and you are anxious most of the time. These are all signs you could have a self-inflicted cuckoo in your nest even though you are passionate about what you are doing. We become driven by our performance instead of driven by our purpose.

Toxic thinking patterns such as overthinking, overanalyzing, and obsessing to the point where we cannot make simple decisions as well as feeling overwhelmed and losing our peace and joy are self-inflicted cuckoos. These toxic patterns create an illness of introspection where we live in our minds rather than in our behaviors. This paralysis-by-analysis mentality keeps us stuck and trapped in cuckoo land, believing the lies we tell ourselves. Toxic-thinking cuckoos suck the joy out of our work, relationships, and life. Simple things become extremely complicated and crippling as we imagine worst-case scenarios and rehearse conversations with people to seek some type of control. However, the more we try to control our circumstances, the more out of control we feel.

Regardless of what your self-inflicted cuckoo might be, you do not realize it is in your nest, yet eventually you become your own worst enemy. The most important thing to understand about the self-inflicted cuckoo is this: you deceive yourself into believing these behaviors will protect you. Your unconscious mind seeks to protect you from feeling pain or experiencing failure and rejection by keeping you in predictable, familiar patterns. Although self-inflicted cuckoos help you feel better in the short term, they are imposters that leave you feeling worse because those patterns are harmful, not helpful. You become consumed by feelings of inadequacy, low self-esteem, and shame as you strive to perform, please, and perfect your life away.

Think of self-inflicted cuckoos as self-erected prisons holding you hostage—you are a prisoner of your own insatiable appetite—yet the door to your prison is open although you do not realize you are free. Hence the nature of the cuckoo. They are sneaky. They resemble what you want. They look as if they belong in your nest, your life. But they are imposters. Remember, the process is subtle at first and you are deceived into thinking things are OK, especially because the self-inflicted cuckoos appear to be good things on the outside. Not until later do you realize you are being held captive by the things, and your true purpose never manifests at all or does not reach its fullness. Essentially your own eggs never hatch and don't come to life, and you have a nest full of imposter eggs that mimic what you want but are not truly what satisfies your heart's deepest desires. Something is missing in your life, and you can't quite put your finger on it. Until now.

The Root of the Self-Inflicted Cuckoo

We are often our own worst enemy because of these self-destructive tendencies and habits we do not acknowledge and refuse to quit. This is because self-inflicted cuckoos are often a symptom of a deeper-rooted issue that needs to be recognized and addressed. This is the time to be honest with yourself, others, and God about the true source of your pain that is hiding beneath the empty promises of your self-inflicted cuckoo.

Self-inflicted cuckoos are a distraction and deceitfully promise to protect you against painful emotions or a fear of failure, rejection, and abandonment. A wounded heart full of fear and unmet relational needs will direct you toward other things to fulfill and satisfy you.

Self-inflicted cuckoos seek to satisfy you when you experience perceived feelings of failure, loneliness, boredom, shame, or disappointment within yourself. Perhaps you lost your best friend, you're recently divorced, your child left home for the first time, your husband is working all the time, or you were diagnosed with an illness.

Maybe you had a painful breakup and turned to shopping as a distraction, and like the cuckoo, it grew bigger and bigger, and now you are making poor financial decisions. Or you turned to binge-watching shows when you lost your job so you could avoid feeling afraid, and now you are spending an inordinate amount of time watching shows and procrastinating about looking for a new job. Or you started a new company and began comparing yourself to people on social media who had a bigger platform, and you lost your passion and joy. You are trying to please an audience based on what others are doing and lost your unique voice as a result, and now you are doubting your purpose altogether. Or you are checking your online dating profile incessantly and neglecting your current relationships with your family, church, and friends because you feel ashamed of being single. At night you have one more glass of wine, and now you cannot go to sleep without it or attend social functions in a sober state.

What are your self-inflicted cuckoos? List them here:

_____

_____

_____

We all have self-inflicted cuckoos. It is part of being human. We each have underlying wounds that await God's grace and truth to cleanse and to heal. It is important to give ourselves grace and have self-compassion as we learn to identify and let go of these destructive behaviors and toxic thinking patterns. Know deep down the truth that we are loved, worthy, successful, needed, and wanted. As we go through the healing process, it is important to give ourselves permission not to do the healing process perfectly. Even if we have moments where we spend too much time online or have too many glasses of wine, it is OK. We can always make a new choice next time the opportunity presents itself to say no to our self-inflicted cuckoo and to say yes to feeling the pain of that moment and realize we do not need to fear the pain any longer and hide from it.

An Invisible Enemy Becomes Visible

Being unable to point our finger to the suffering we experience is one of the most painful experiences a person can encounter day after day. For this reason, the Cuckoo Syndrome represents an invisible, self-destructive pattern and a compilation of symptoms that hides from your awareness until you find a name for it.

Regardless of whether you have an unhealthy relationship cuckoo or a self-inflicted cuckoo, the Cuckoo Syndrome is an imposter and a counterfeit purpose.

Whether you are hosting the relationship cuckoo or the self-inflicted cuckoo, they are an invisible enemy, a blind spot. You do not know they are right in front of you. As stated, they are initially disguised as a good thing or a healthy person, or else you wouldn't find yourself in this dynamic in the first place; you would have known right away.

Think of the Cuckoo Syndrome as an autoimmune disease that is not always visible even though the internal pain exists. The body mistakenly attacks itself. The disease is weakening the body and creating internal damage. This is similar to a cancer in which the rapid creation of abnormal cells invades the body and has the potential to spread throughout. I have had many clients who were suffering from chronic pain who said they felt as if they had an invisible disease. The earlier these diseases can be detected, the sooner treatment can begin. And so it is with the Cuckoo Syndrome.

The Cuckoo Syndrome exists beneath the surface; its invisible wound and associated pain erode your strength, hope, and purpose. Eventually you find yourself in a conundrum, depleted, shattered, exhausted, and believing it is too late. You find yourself more and more in the constant company of anxiety, stress, depression, and addiction. Hidden within your soul is lingering confusion, insecurity, and fear that haunt you about your needs, wants, and desires.

Breaking free from the Cuckoo Syndrome starts by bringing this invisible enemy to light by naming who or what your cuckoo is and how you allow it to show up in your life. We spend a significant portion of our lives fighting the wrong enemy, hiding from our true selves, and wondering why we continue to remain stuck and unfulfilled. It is largely because the real source of the problem is invisible to us.

Much of our lack of awareness is contributing to our cycle of suffering. This realization is not an easy one, and it is not pain-free, but living your life according to the cuckoo's demands and rules is certainly not a pain-free process either. Just because you are aware of the cuckoo dynamics in your life, relational or self-inflicted, they will not automatically disappear, but they will no longer remain hidden and powerful. The healing process requires hard work and facing the true source of your pain in conjunction with God's help and the help of others so that freedom and wholeness arise.

Addressing this invisible enemy and its associated wounds allow the healing process to begin. As you recover the lost parts of yourself, new energy awaits you because you are no longer allowing the cuckoo to dictate your happiness, steal your purpose, run your life, and drain your energy. Hope for your dreams and heart's desires that were smothered by the cuckoo is rediscovered and reignited. Your relationships improve as the toxic stronghold of the cuckoo struggle loosens its grip over your life so you are no longer held captive.

CHAPTER 2

STUCK IN CUCKOO LAND

How to Deal with the Cuckoos in Your Life

Keep away from people who try to belittle your ambitions. Small people always do that, but the really great make you feel that you, too, can become great.
—MARK TWAIN

YOU HAVE TALKED TO EVERYONE—YOUR FRIENDS, YOUR family, your pastor, your small group members, your mentor, your coworkers, and even a counselor—yet you remain stuck. Your intuition, your sense of discernment, and your gut are all telling you something is not right. You know the behavior of your cuckoo is not OK, yet you have neither a full understanding nor the tools to deal with this unhealthy relationship. You have come to the right place. It is time to dive deep and provide you with a helpful strategy for breaking free from the cuckoo's snare.

The Cuckoo-Host Struggle

Research shows that some species of host birds can defend themselves against cuckoos: "Hosts are not just passive victims; they fight back, because the costs of being conned are tremendously high."[11] Hosts can aggressively attack adult female cuckoos and prevent them from invading their nests.

Defend yourself and make it difficult for a cuckoo to deceive you and commit to learning the tools for identifying and rejecting their advances. Your first defense is to fight back by using your voice effectively, expressing your needs, and setting boundaries. An additional line of defense is to distinguish your eggs so they are not prone to being destroyed by imposters. Hosts can make it difficult for cuckoos to mimic their eggs by producing eggs with intricate designs, marks, and signatures.

You, too, can protect your eggs by making them unique. The more your eggs look like you, the more secure your eggs are. Do not just accept a counterfeit cuckoo egg because taking care of it will become your life's purpose and will replace your purpose. (Chapters 12, 13, and 14 of this book will serve as a guide to secure your "eggs," which are your purpose, passions, and heart's desires.)

I explain to my clients that when dealing with a cuckoo, initially there is an inevitable and constant battle and struggle to defend yourself and essentially protect your nest. It is time to guard your heart and stand strong. This is a process, and it requires hard emotional work. But you will no longer succumb to the costly work of taking care of the cuckoos and giving your life away to them.

An evolutionary biologist who studies parasitic birds (such as cuckoos) stated, "It's an ever-changing race as to how to fool the host birds, since they too evolve in response."[12] The cuckoos in your life are evolving as you evolve because they are thinking of ways to fool and manipulate you once you catch on to their toxic behavior. They come up with a backup plan and aim to be one step ahead of you.

Remember, cuckoo birds use strategies such as trickery and deceit to outsmart their victims. You do not have to be a victim of a cuckoo. Despite a human cuckoo's deceitful agenda to prey on your vulnerabilities to use and take advantage of you, it is possible to learn to identify their various disguises and manipulative behavior. You can prevent this person from invading your life by not allowing yourself to be their "host" and becoming involved in a cuckoo relationship. The more you learn to fight back, the less vulnerable you are to being the target of a cuckoo.

Five Beginning Steps on How to Deal with the Cuckoos in Your Life

The following model presents an overview. Each chapter deals with these steps in different ways as a particular cuckoo sweeps in and begins its deceitful actions.

- Honor your reality. Be honest with yourself and face the truth.
- Stop doing their work. Switch the focus from them to you.
- Set boundaries and use your voice effectively.

- Validate your emotions and express your needs.
- Seek professional help. Create a strategy with knowledge-able experts.

Honor Your Reality: Be Honest with Yourself and Face the Truth

Cuckoos seek to establish a dynamic where you question your reality and sanity through their process of manipulation, deceit, and control. I want to encourage you by noting that even the brightest, most self-aware people can be deceived by a cuckoo.

A recurring theme in this book is this: We suffer when we avoid truth or reality. We suffer when we avoid facing the truth of our cuckoo-related pain. People are often too afraid to feel their pain because they do not know how to deal with something so overwhelming.

The cuckoo dynamic in our lives creates such a profound distortion of the truth. Therefore we become vulnerable to believing the cuckoo's lies and consequently cannot see the reality of their harmful behavior. Similarly, defending the cuckoo's behavior by lying to ourselves further blocks the truth that we are continually being hurt. For example, you might find yourself rationalizing, *It's not so bad, Things could be worse, They are going through a hard time right now. They are not trying to hurt me.* All the while, we are ignoring our feelings, suffering silently, and suffocating under the toxic weight of the cuckoo.

The first step in honoring your reality is to be honest with yourself. Give yourself a reality check: Ask yourself questions such as, *What am I really experiencing? Am I being lied to? Is something seriously wrong here? What are my gut and intuition telling me? Is something not OK? What is missing from my life?*

In addition to not defending the cuckoo's behavior, you must refrain from defending yourself to your cuckoo. Even though they are constantly questioning your every move, accusing you of things you have not done, or twisting your words, stop defending yourself because it is covering up their dysfunctional behavior. Become very quiet, listen, and pay attention to how you feel when they speak to you. Is what they are saying based in reality or is it packaged in a lie?

Before the truth can set you free, you must identify what lies are holding you captive. Cuckoos aim to fool us, but we can fool ourselves too. When we lie to ourselves long enough, we begin to believe those lies, especially when we are afraid and trying to escape pain. When we cling to these lies, they are what become the origin of greater suffering.

Facing the truth that we are hosting a cuckoo relationship allows us to accept reality and let go of the lies we are told by the cuckoo and the lies we tell ourselves. We must devote ourselves to facing the deepest truths we have avoided in our relationships. As a result, we can get unstuck and stop saying *yes* when we really mean *no*.

Reach out to a safe person you can trust. Tell your story and your truth without worrying what the cuckoo will say or think. Keep your conversations with this person private. It is time to hear an objective, reality-based perspective and begin identifying false narratives instead of listening to the cuckoo's lies. Cuckoos build a case against you with other people in your life, and they want you to question yourself. They might say, "Your friends also know how sensitive you are about everything." They want you to feel alone and to isolate you. Your isolation from friends and family feeds their control over you and significantly alters your reality.

Just because you see the reality, do not fall into another trap of trying to get your cuckoo to see it too. That trap will just create another cuckoo, Cuckoo 2.0, because those all-consuming, crazy-making conversations will leave you wondering if you are wrong.

Stop Doing Their Work: Switch the Focus from Them to You

The first step in switching the focus from them to you is to stop trying to convince the cuckoo of their hurtful behavior. It is best to begin by focusing on your own needs and pain to begin the process of healing.

Like the host parent, you are being deceived by a cuckoo who is a toxic taker and you are the giver.

Here is a summary up to this point of how cuckoos operate in relationships:

- A cuckoo has no strength of its own.
- A cuckoo is a parasite. It lives on a host.
- The host is *you.*
- The host feeds the cuckoo.
- The cuckoo causes harm to its host.
- The cuckoo grows bigger and bigger as you feed it.
- You did not know the cuckoo is right in front of you. Now you do.
- Stop doing their work. You must do work on you.

Switching the focus to yourself is not selfish; it helps you overcome your tendency to put your cuckoo's needs above your own. Here are some questions to ask yourself: *How do I feel? What do I think? What do I need? What do I want? What is my body experiencing?* Then validate your emotions and have compassion on yourself. Share your feelings and thoughts with your cuckoo. Do you feel known, loved, and cared for by them?

Do you find yourself wondering, *What did I used to think about myself before this cuckoo dropped into my life? Who am I? What do I enjoy doing? What eggs (hopes and dreams) have been taken from my nest?*

Take a moment and write the answers here:

_____

_____

_____

Know your inner passions and your heart's deepest desires. The cuckoo will never make it about you, so you have to make it about you.

Give yourself the same emotional energy, time, and attention you have given to your cuckoo. There has been too much focus on feeding (taking care of) the cuckoo in your nest while your eggs are suffocating. It is not a mutual relationship. Is this person investing their time and energy to genuinely change?

The cuckoo does not want to do the work. The cuckoo wants you to do the work for them. You feel responsible for your cuckoo. Feeling responsible for another person is a major signal that you have a cuckoo in your nest. These responsibilities include financial, spiritual, social, mental, physical, or relational.

The cuckoo tries to convince you that you owe them your time, energy, and attention. They use you for your kindness and generosity. The more you give of yourself to them, the more they will take from you. Resist this temptation and be strong regardless of how badly they treat you. It is important to develop new and healthy patterns.

Cuckoos have adopted a *learned helplessness* attitude and lifestyle. Learned helplessness occurs when the cuckoo convinces themselves they do not have the ability to change a circumstance. Instead, they manipulate other people to help them fix a situation for them. They do not have to face the reality of their circumstances. They develop a victim mentality.

Cuckoos hold you hostage. They could be dealing with a chronic illness or sickness, a financial crisis, or a mental health issue, and they want you to take care of them and fix their situation. They try to manipulate you through passive-aggressive behavior or threaten you in some way to make your life miserable until you rescue them.

Many of my clients ask, "What do I say to them?" I tell them not to expend energy and time trying to figure out what to say to their cuckoo because the cuckoo does not want to understand. Instead of trying to convince them, work on letting go of feeling responsible. Ask yourself, *What do I want my relationship with them to be?*

Do not get into a dialogue with your cuckoo about solving their problems. Refrain from giving them answers. Instead, listen and empathize by saying such things as, "That must be hard." Also, suggest other people who can help them: a counselor, a pastor, an attorney, a mentor, a financial advisor, a doctor, a psychiatrist, a personal trainer, a nutritionist. Cuckoos want to be rescued and lifted out of their difficult circumstances altogether. By suggesting other people who can help them, you are removing yourself from the equation and refusing to take on responsibility for the cuckoo.

Look at the reed warbler feeding the cuckoo chick at the beginning of this chapter. By comparison, the cuckoo is an enormous, grotesque chick. What do you feel toward the reed warbler? Now direct these emotions toward yourself.

Do you experience empathy and compassion for the reed warbler, which is exhausting itself feeding the cuckoo chick's insatiable appetite, not knowing it is not even their chick? Meanwhile their own eggs are being suffocated and will never hatch or come to life! Perhaps you feel sad, heartbroken, and angry at the cuckoo chick.

What do you feel? Take a moment and write down these emotions:

_____

_____

_____

If you could speak to the reed warbler, what truth would you tell the warbler about what is really going on? Perhaps, "Something is wrong and not OK," or, "You are being used, taken advantage of, and deceived," or, "You have an imposter in your nest that doesn't belong!"

Now think of what truth you would say to yourself about your cuckoo. Write it here:

_____

_____

_____

As you look at the cuckoo chick in the illustration, what do you feel toward it? Anger perhaps? What do you want to say or do with the cuckoo chick? Now think of what you want to say or do with the cuckoo in your life. Write your answers below:

_____

_____

_____

_____

Pain, fear, anger, sadness, and grief linger beneath the cuckoo in your nest.

Throughout the day, repeat this exercise and take the time to put the focus back on you.

Set Boundaries and Use Your Voice Effectively

The next step is establishing healthy boundaries to ensure you do not repeat the cuckoo cycle and revert to living in cuckoo land. Being tangled up in a cuckoo relationship with no boundaries is a signal to you that the relationship is unhealthy. Boundaries are a key component to healing. Most people have been conditioned to please others and perform a role such as the family peacemaker since childhood. The result is that we abandon ourselves.

If you are deeply entangled and entrapped in an unhealthy, inappropriate emotional relationship with another person who uses and takes advantage of you, you need some boundaries. For example, a parent might create an emotional dynamic where they get their relational and emotional needs and their sense of security from their children instead of their spouse.

In my private practice I have witnessed this dynamic. Even as a married adult with their own families, my clients still feel a sense of obligation to take care of their mother or father emotionally and/or physically. They feel guilty and selfish if they put their spouse and children above the needs of their adult parents.

Chronic caretaking by putting others above self is exhausting, lopsided, draining, and costly. Therefore they develop the following false beliefs:

> *"If I connect to people and have a relationship with them, they will take from me."*

"Being in a relationship means I am responsible for another person."

Then one of the following corresponding relational patterns usually develops because of these false beliefs:

- They attract more cuckoos into their life who are takers instead of givers.
- They suffer by avoiding people and relationships altogether and end up being alone or lack closeness and intimacy in their relationships because they withhold who they really are and what they want.

This saddens me because they are missing out on experiencing healthy, mutual relationships with kind and giving people who reciprocate instead of carrying the weight and heavy burden of the cuckoo in their life.

In summary:

A Cuckoo Relationship = Tangled Entrapped Thoughts and Feelings
= False Beliefs about Responsibility
= Exhausting and Costly Behaviors
= Eggs That Never Hatch (Purpose and Dreams Never Manifest)

During the treatment process of helping my clients set boundaries with their cuckoo, I explain to them that they will need to break away and have some space to gain insight on how to end this unhealthy pattern of relating. For example, the client can say to the cuckoo, "If I seem unavailable for a time and I am more quiet than usual and do not spend as much time seeing you, it's because I am working out some personal things in my life and need some space. I will let you know when I am ready to get together with you again." Do not give any more detail or explanation.

In my treatment of clients, I share the following truth when we arrive at this portion of their treatment process: "If you feel guilty and selfish, that is how you know you are on the right path."

This is because as you begin to set boundaries and use your voice, you may feel initially guilty and selfish. Take that as a sign that you are on the right path. Part of the healing process is to overcome those lies you have been told repeatedly by the cuckoo that you have come to believe are true. The familiar pattern has been to lose yourself under their controlling demands and feel self-centered or selfish when you try to speak up for yourself.

You do not need them to acknowledge your pain to heal and break free. Being misunderstood or even accused is part of the healing process. They will not always understand your boundaries, but that doesn't mean you are doing something wrong.

What Does It Look Like to Set a Boundary and Use Your Voice Effectively?

Setting a boundary is more of an action or behavior change on your part. For example, stop doing everything for them. Perhaps it is the carpool, the grocery, the lawn, babysitting, car maintenance, the investments, the bill budgeting, talking to extended family, playing with the children, or doing the homework or household chores.

Good boundaries are objective, simple, and clear. In any given conversation or situation, stating our limitations allow us to stay in tune with our needs, including the inner voice of our intuition.

Having a voice is just as it sounds: use your words. For example, start by saying *no*. Voice your needs. Say how you feel. Say what you think. Say want you want. Give your opinion even if it is not noticed.

Hold your boundaries. Recognize that people who do not respect your boundaries don't want to understand them and therefore cannot honor them. Be consistent. Be strong. Stand your ground no matter what reaction you receive or how selfish or guilty you might feel. Remember, their arguments are not grounded in reality. They distort the truth.

Listen to your inner voice, your intuition. It takes time to establish your voice of authenticity and be true to yourself. Operating from this place allows room for you to hear God's still, small voice so you can receive his wisdom about you and your situation.

You create another cuckoo as you argue with yourself about being firm and decisive. This cycle creates an additional layer of unnecessary suffering.

For example, if your cuckoo constantly says, "I miss you. I never see you or talk to you enough," you can respond, "I am talking to you/spending time with you now. Why don't we enjoy this time together?" Or, "I only have twenty minutes to talk."

This boundary prevents you from having to spend too much time with them, from participating in unhealthy emotional intimacy, and from allowing them to get too close for the purpose of taking advantage of you.

When someone is trying to force their opinion on you or engage in conversation that feels emotionally inappropriate, boundaries can sound like the following:

"I am not asking for feedback right now."

"I need time to think on that. I'll respond when and if I am ready."

In my work with clients, I've found the following boundaries are helpful when dealing with a cuckoo relationship in your life:

- You are allowed to have a voice.
- You are allowed to walk away.
- You are not the rescuer of every crisis.
- You are allowed to disagree.
- You do not need to defend yourself.
- You do not need to explain every situation.
- You do not need to give a reason.
- You are allowed to have space.

Due to their extreme woundedness, cuckoos filter every interaction with you through a lens of rejection. Unhealthy people are extremely defensive. Because they perceive rejection, they develop a strong sense of entitlement. They believe it is their right because they believe you have wronged them.

It is important to note that you can forgive them, but forgiveness does not always equate to a relationship. This is especially true when the other person does not show a repentant heart and is not willing to acknowledge or take responsibility for their actions.

The cuckoo's biggest identifier is control. The cuckoo displays anger when you set a boundary and have a voice because they fear they are losing control over you. They get furious when you set a boundary or say *no* because it rubs up against their selfish agendas. They will punish you directly by trying to get you to feel wrong, guilty, ashamed, or selfish; give you the silent treatment; verbally abuse you; blame you; or become passive aggressive. Cuckoos operate from a position of shame, usually from earlier wounds that have nothing to do with you, so they go on the attack and cannot take responsibility for themselves or feel empathy toward you. It is not possible to be responsible for carrying the feelings of another person because they do not belong to you in the first place.

Here is an example of a client who was not using her voice or setting the appropriate boundaries. She was doing all the work and called it sacrifice when the reality was that she was not honoring her own needs in the relationship with her sister.

Christine came for counseling due to anxiety and feeling stuck because of a challenging relationship with her younger sister, Sarah. She had two sisters and was very close with her other sister, Mary, whom she considered a best friend. After spending time with Sarah, she would feel drained and emotionally exhausted, but she couldn't put her finger on why. It took many sessions to help her understand that her anxiety was a symptom that was masking her real emotion of anger toward Sarah.

She felt guilty for preferring spending time with Mary over Sarah. Christine hesitantly admitted, "I leave my time with Sarah feeling hurt and confused. I just don't enjoy her company." She felt trapped because she believed she had to make the sacrifice and spend quality one-on-one time with Sarah as she did with Mary. This is because Sarah would constantly compare the two relationships and say, "Why do you always answer Mary's calls and not mine?" "You text Mary more than you do me." "You have not invited me over to your place in a while, but Mary was there last week." "Why do you tell Mary things about your life and not me?"

Out of guilt, Christine would make excuses because she knew Sarah was right, but she did not know how to handle it honestly without hurting Sarah's feelings. Even in our session, Christine was taking responsibility for Sarah's emotions at the expense of her own.

Sarah had recently lashed out at Christine for spending time with Mary. When Christine responded by sharing her feelings in a respectful way, Sarah ignored her feelings completely and lashed out again.

It was then that Christine realized Sarah was not a safe person; she only cared about her own feelings, and this was a long-standing pattern. Christine felt a tinge of anger and was quite shaken.

At the same time, Christine felt confused because she understood Sarah's feelings of rejection and said, "I feel guilty because I know she just wants to spend more time together. Shouldn't I just make the sacrifice? She is my sister, after all."

Christine made plenty of sacrifices over the years, and it was never good enough for Sarah. Her extended family was also quite close and would get together often. Christine was making sacrifices such as spending time with Sarah at family gatherings. But Christine couldn't see that. The relationship proved to be hurtful and exhausting; it was always about Sarah's needs and Sarah's feelings.

Christine was turning her anger back on herself rather than giving herself permission to be angry toward Sarah.

"Do you think Sarah is spending the time and money in counseling concerned with your feelings the way you are with hers?" I asked Christine.

"Absolutely not," she replied. "She would never do that because she only thinks about herself."

I said, "So it sounds like you are saying Sarah does not take your feelings into consideration, and she operates from a place of self-pity when she talks to you?"

Christine was able to see how her anxiety and feeling of being trapped in the relationship were masking her anger.

It took her some time to allow herself to feel that anger toward Sarah because she was protecting Sarah's feelings even in our counseling session.

We did a role-play scenario in which I was Sarah.

"Well, you just prefer Mary over me," I said.

I stopped the role play and asked Christine, "What would you want to say back to Sarah honestly, without fearing her response?"

Christine said confidently, "Yes, there is truth to that because you have broken my trust many times and have never sincerely apologized. I also don't feel safe to share my feelings with you because you shut me down. Therefore, our relationship is not mutual since you dump all your feelings on me and do not give me the same respect."

Christine felt freedom and relief acknowledging the truth that her relationships with her sisters were not at all the same. She felt a newfound permission to pursue her relationship with her other sister, Mary, free of fear and without taking responsibility for Sarah's reaction and feelings.

At a deeper level, she realized her thoughts about Sarah were stealing the joy from her beautiful relationship with Mary. Christine chose to spend time with Sarah solely during family functions and holidays because the relationship was not one of mutual respect and she could not trust Sarah with her heart. There was no emotional intimacy.

I've discovered when dealing with clients who display these types of unhealthy behaviors that it is crucial to note people are responsible for their own emotions and for communicating them to you in a way that you know they are genuine. And until that happens, you are free to live and enjoy your life. How do you know if that is not the case? You will walk away from a conversation with that person feeling unheard, manipulated, guilty, confused, and perhaps a little crazy. They have a way of *complicating* the simple and *twisting* facts into an emotional mess.

If Sarah actually wanted to sit down with Christine and say, "I notice that we are not as close as I hoped we could be, and I would really like to understand why our relationship is not as intimate as the one you have with Mary," Christine might feel safe enough to be honest and explain in a loving way so Sarah could begin to make amends. However, Sarah made comparisons and sly, critical remarks to get her emotions across without caring about Christine's feelings.

It is important not to sacrifice your time for someone if there is no trust, no mutual respect, no reciprocation, or no compassion for your feelings. Honor your God-given emotion of anger to motivate you to set a boundary, have a voice, be honest, and take care of yourself. The other person is most likely not lying awake at night thinking about you, paying for counseling sessions to consider your feelings, or experiencing inner turmoil over how to communicate with you. The person most in control in this dynamic is the one who cares the least.

Validate Your Emotions and Express Your Needs

Validating your emotions means being honest with yourself about what you are feeling and learning how to honor your feelings. An essential component of your true self that has been lost in your cuckoo relationship is your emotions. Most of us go through life disconnected from our true selves and unaware of who we are, what we feel, what we want, and what we need. This is largely due to our childhoods, when we were taught, implicitly or explicitly, by our parents and caregivers to ignore or deny our needs and feelings in order to gain acceptance or avoid punishment.

We develop a pattern of pleasing, performing, and protecting our family dynamics, which ultimately leads to an abandonment of self. This cycle creates an undercurrent of suffering underlying issues because our needs go unmet for prolonged periods and our true self erodes. Therefore, it is imperative that we learn to find ourselves again or else we find ourselves again identifying false narratives we believe to be true, such as, "My needs and feelings are not worthy of being me" or "I am a burden to others." These false beliefs can attract unhealthy people who want to use us and take advantage of our willingness to chronically neglect ourselves. We become vulnerable to cuckoos.

Unhealthy people invalidate your emotions. They do not acknowledge the feelings you express in the relationship; they repeatedly dismiss them. They punish you instead of caring for you and nurturing your feelings in a healthy way. They tie up their own emotions with yours, and you are left without a separate identity. You feel disoriented because you are consistently told your emotions are not true or real and, worse, that your emotions hurt them!

You have the right to feel what you are feeling. We each have our own emotional compass to help guide us to know our personal values and an inner sense of what is right or wrong for us. Your emotional life is your responsibility, because no one else can tell you what to feel or what not to feel.

My clients will often apologize when they begin to cry or say, "I'm sorry for being so negative." My goal in counseling is to help them feel their feelings rather than feel guilty or ashamed that their emotions are unhealthy or wrong. Some feel they are burdening me with their emotions.

As a child, when expressing emotions, our parents' responses to our emotions might be:

"That hurts me that you would say that."

"You are criticizing me."

"You don't care about me or you wouldn't feel that way."

"You are being selfish."

"You are being insensitive."

"You are disrespecting me."

Essentially, in our adult cuckoo relationships, the cuckoo twists your emotions and makes it about them, and they usually get defensive rather than trying to understand. These responses lead to pain and confusion because the child, and later the adult, either doubts themselves, people pleases, numbs their feelings, or becomes overwhelmed by intense rage.

If your mother or father manipulated you to get what they wanted by dumping their emotions onto you, your own emotional compass is skewed. If your caregivers blamed you for their issues, you may find it confusing to know how to separate your issues from that of your cuckoo.

What does having a cuckoo in your nest feel like?

- Grief, lost parts of yourself and your dreams
- Pervasive guilt that you cannot put your finger on
- Shame, always feeling as if you are doing something wrong
- Rejected, unloved, and no longer cherished, pursued, or cared for
- Sadness, a chronic sensation of emptiness
- Fear, walking around with a cloud of dread hanging over you all the time
- You feel anger but you cannot show it

What are your needs?

When we do not know what our needs are, we do not know how to communicate them or how to meet our needs in healthy ways. Our needs tell us the truth about ourselves; therefore, when we do not trust ourselves and our ability to make decisions, we struggle to trust God to guide us to truth. The healing process entails becoming aware of our own needs.

Start by asking yourself, *What do I need right now, in this moment?* If you are having difficulty locating your needs, identify what you are feeling. Listen to your body. For example, do you have a headache or muscle tension (perhaps you are stressed), are your palms sweaty, is your heart racing, do you have butterflies in your stomach (perhaps you are anxious)? Take a moment to write down what you need in a journal so you can practice putting words to your needs. For example, maybe you feel too tired to go to Bible study tonight. Instead, choose to stay home, get into your pajamas, watch your favorite television show, make that recipe you've been wanting to try, or take a bubble bath. This way you are honoring your need to rest and recharge.

It takes courage to share your needs. Communicating your needs to another person allows them to acknowledge who you are and also exposes cuckoo dynamics in unhealthy relationships where there is a lack of reciprocity. A person who loves you unconditionally will give you the space, permission, and freedom to be yourself. They will understand your deepest hurts, validate you, show compassion, and take ownership of their role in the relationship. There will exist a mutual interest in meeting one another's needs, and each person will feel safe, heard, and known in each other's presence.

We will explore ways to address your emotions and find healing in chapter 3, "The Cuckoo of Not Feeling Your Feelings."

Seek Professional Help: Create a Strategy with Knowledgeable Experts

Many clients who are in abusive and unhealthy relationships ask me if that person will ever change, get better, or heal. My response is, "People can change, but you cannot change them."

I am not disregarding the fact that people can change if they are willing to do the work, but the person has to exert their own will in this process and actually want help. These individuals have a tendency to jump from counselor to counselor once the counselor begins to expose their behavior. They can also be brilliant with their words and charismatic, and manipulate even therapists into believing they have changed. They can view therapy as something to check off their list or to appease you or use it as an opportunity to build a case about how they are right and "you are the one with all the issues." I advise my clients who are in cuckoo relationships to determine whether the person is willing to change their behaviors and take responsibility for their actions.

The person might say they really do want to change, but time will tell if their actions correspond to their words. The crucial element is for you to do your part by setting boundaries and using your voice effectively in the relationship. If you do those behaviors, you are going to find out whether they will change or not.

I am also asked, "How can you heal destructive family situations when they do not believe they need healing or have not acknowledged they have done anything wrong?" You cannot heal these family issues without active participation from each person. But you can heal and make changes with God's help and the help of others, which will shift how you operate within your family.

Now that you have identified you are in a cuckoo relationship, you're probably wondering, *Do I stay in the relationship or leave?* At this point, determining the answer is premature. For now, learning to actively put into practice the five steps in this chapter will ultimately assist you in making a choice that is healthy and best for you. Following these steps by taking action will move you toward an answer to the question of staying or leaving.

My goal is to help you make the choice of staying or leaving relationships but not from a place of being stuck.

It is not about *what* decision you are making; it is about the process of *how* you are arriving at a decision to stay or go and how you carry it out. As mentioned in step two, you must do the work for you and stop doing the work of the cuckoo.

The upcoming chapters in this book will reveal the necessary truths so you can do the healing work in your own life first. As you grow and learn the truth, freedom emerges, and you can make major relational decisions from a place of empowerment and faith, not powerlessness and fear.

There's more to come on how to discover the answer to the staying-or-leaving question in chapter 9, "Cuckoo Counsel: Who Hurts You and Who Can Help You." That chapter will also address how to find a good counselor, what questions to ask, what the best strategies are, what to say to the other person about counseling, and what to expect in counseling. It includes signs for how to watch out for cuckoo tactics where deception and manipulation make their way into the counseling session.

If you find yourself in a difficult and exhausting relationship with a cuckoo and feel stuck, I encourage you to seek help from a professional counselor to assist you in the process of advocating for your needs, using your voice effectively, setting boundaries, and expressing your emotions in a safe and compassionate environment. You also can learn specific tools on how to deal with the unhealthy relationship, whether it is through minimal contact or no contact to prevent further pain or abuse.

It is important to note that even healthy relationships have times of struggle, heartache, and discord. In a healthy relationship, both people have a mutual desire to address conflict and honor one another's experience in the relationship. If the relationship is lopsided, and only one person is doing the work, ultimately the persistent imbalance will erode the relationship and suffering becomes the core of the relationship.

Understanding the nature of cuckoo relational dynamics is crucial because your responsibility and energy have been twisted to meet their ever-demanding, insatiable, never-satisfied wants and needs. Up until now this cycle has been familiar and comfortable to you. Once you begin to find yourself again, your energy will be redirected to those things and those people who invigorate you, and self-confidence will no longer be a foreign experience. Your relationships become less exhausting and burdensome, and you no longer must isolate and hide parts of who you are to please another.

Ultimately you will learn to avoid lopsided relationships, to understand how they bring suffering instead of joy, and to enjoy the fulfillment of what it means to be truly known and loved unconditionally. Knowing the difference between a cuckoo relationship and a healthy relationship is tricky. Having a counselor can help you make this distinction. The counseling process can bring clarity to the question of whether it is time to leave, including romantic relationships, jobs, friendships, or a church.

Being in an unhealthy relationship with a cuckoo enables your dreams, desires, passions, and purpose to get smothered and die. In the final chapter of this book, "Let Your Eggs Hatch! Treasures from Darkness," we will explore how to take back what has been stolen from your nest and never allowed to hatch. The good news is there is hope. It is never too late to be proactive and to take the necessary steps to obtain freedom.

The Cuckoo in My Nest

One of my fondest memories from my childhood was a game my family called "Lion," where my dad would get on his knees and wave his hands and roar loudly while my siblings and I would feverishly run around the house and wait for him to catch and tickle us. My father was like the Great Gatsby in terms of his personality, looks, and charisma. He enjoyed throwing parties, was a great dresser, and was intelligent, witty, and fun. He was my dad. Growing up, he created a profoundly fun dynamic in our home. Yet he also had a very destructive part of himself that was confusing and devastating to me. His anger grew worse during my childhood and adolescent years. The traumatic, scary moments were mixed in with the good moments. I lived with an undercurrent of fear and dread, not knowing when his rage would be directed toward me, my siblings, or my mother.

When I was growing up, I felt like my father was unable to truly know my suffering or hear the cry of my heart. I felt like the tiny reed warbler in the illustration being consumed by the huge cuckoo. I felt smaller and smaller as my father's emotions got bigger and bigger.

There was always this perplexing dynamic about my relationship with my dad, where I felt as if something was not OK. I could not understand his highly complex personality because many times he was fun-loving, but sometimes he was physically violent and volatile.

In the multitude of counselors there is safety. (PROV. 11:14)

Decades ago, my healing coincided with my parents' divorce, which landed me in counseling during that particularly difficult season of my life. It was not until I began my own journey of personal growth and therapy that I felt safe and was finally able to put a voice to my pain and tell my story.

With time, I realized I couldn't demand answers from my father, so I decided to forgive him. There was no point in trying to right the wrongs and force a genuine apology or have him admit to what he had done. Holding him accountable was only hurting myself. Trying to get him to understand became a cuckoo all on its own. I made the decision that his lack of acknowledgment wouldn't sever our relationship. I decided to settle for a place where I could be at peace with myself, despite all the unsolvable issues. I wanted to be free to love him regardless.

I was in and out of our relationship for many years. Over time I made several attempts to reconnect only to find it continued to be hurtful.

I have always been an intuitive and empathic person, and even as a child I was fascinated by people and had an intense curiosity why they do the things they do. I wanted to help, to hear people's stories, and to understand the human heart. I have much compassion for my father, as I am sure he was suffering in his own ways, and it was never his intention to hurt me, even though he did.

Now, as a professional counselor, I find tremendous joy when I can use my desire to help people understand their heartaches and find rest for their weary souls, and give them a safe place to tell their story.

CHAPTER 3

THE CUCKOO OF NOT FEELING YOUR FEELINGS

What Happens When You Avoid Emotions?

The best and most beautiful things in the world cannot be seen or even touched. They must be felt with the heart.
—Helen Keller

THIS CHAPTER WILL REVEAL AN IN-DEPTH LOOK AT THE powerful role emotions play in motivating us to live out these tools successfully in our daily life. Our feelings are an essential component to dealing with the cuckoos who have invaded our lives. To face our cuckoos, we must first face our feelings.

Buried Emotions: Bringing the Unconscious to Consciousness

Becoming conscious of our feelings gives us a sense of our true self, the foundation of our identity, and who we are in Christ. Feelings also allow us to know ourselves, others, and God authentically in the most intimate way. Feelings reveal to us who we are, what we want, what we do not want, and the choices we make from moment to moment. When we avoid our feelings, we lose the valuable information they provide.

When my clients are not feeling their feelings, they are simultaneously unaware of their needs, wants, and desires, which all serve as a guard against cuckoos taking advantage of them. Therefore, they have difficulty setting healthy boundaries in relationships with the cuckoo in their lives. When we avoid our emotions, we become susceptible to unhealthy relationships and self-sabotaging behaviors. After years in private practice, I am convinced that we all have developed ways to avoid our emotions.

We feel feelings all through every day, whether we are aware of them or not. I encourage my clients to feel their feelings and not fear their feelings. The most important aspect of healing and genuine transformation is to become aware of your buried, unconscious feelings. This process occurs by shifting your attention away from the cuckoos in your life who continually take from you. Now is the time to pay attention to who you are, how you feel, and what your needs are instead of chronically neglecting yourself to please your cuckoo.

What Are Emotions?

Throughout this chapter I use the words *feelings* and *emotions* interchangeably. Essentially, feelings are how we label our emotions. We typically say, "I feel sad" as opposed to "I have an emotion of sadness." Emotions such as anger, sadness, fear, and happiness are hardwired, nondebatable, and biological reactions that occur automatically in our brain and body. Your brain unconsciously evaluates your environment as you experience day-to-day life. These messages are processed in the limbic system of the brain as well as the autonomic nervous system, which is responsible for emotional activity outside our conscious awareness. This process is then motioned through the body, followed by physiological changes such as increased heart rate and respiration. Our emotions can also be expressed through our body language and facial expressions.

All of this is to say that I've found many people falsely believe that having emotions is a choice. They say, "I shouldn't feel this way" or, worse, "Emotions are sinful." Emotions are neither good nor bad, right nor wrong; they simply *are*. We do have a choice whether we feel our feelings or avoid them. Understanding and processing your emotions as they arise and dealing with the associated thoughts and behaviors in a healthy, productive manner can bring healing and wholeness.

I've discovered in my work with clients that their emotions serve as an inner compass to guide and inform them of impending threats and how to protect themselves. If we are created with emotions to guide us in helpful ways, why do we frequently avoid them? In short, because they are painful and scary. Clients do not come into counseling saying, "My issue is that I am avoiding my emotions" or, "I am afraid of feeling my feelings of sadness or anger." They are suffering with things such as unhappy marriages, burnout, addictions, and financial struggles.

We do not bury our emotions consciously, logically, or rationally because this can happen on autopilot. Even though we ignore, deny, or numb our emotions, they are still active and alive inside us, lingering beneath the surface and creating unnecessary suffering.

How Do We Learn to Avoid Our Emotions?

Based on my clinical experiences, I've noticed that many of the problems clients come to counseling to address (depression, anxiety, stress, loneliness, and relationship difficulties) are rooted in the ways people have learned to fear and avoid their emotions. Ninety percent of this learning is unconscious. Unconscious means beyond conscious awareness. It is a fancy word for *buried*, whether it is burying our pain, unpleasant emotions, or traumatic memories, all of which are understandably so hard and scary to feel.

We always have feelings; we just learn to hide them from other people. Due to our past experiences, we come to believe we are not allowed to say no or be angry, afraid, vulnerable, or imperfect. This learning can occur in past relationships (e.g., romantic, friendships), during childhood experiences with our primary caregivers, teachings in church that emotions are not OK, or a combination of any or all of these. Therefore, expressing our feelings can trigger anxiety. If sharing feelings was dangerous in a past relationship, the body acts as if it is still dangerous in present relationships. If we learned to hide our feelings in the past, we might do so today. Hiding feelings may have been helpful in those moments; it may have alleviated some anxiety, but doing so now creates problems and symptoms that lead to unnecessary suffering. Anxiety is a signal of an underlying buried emotion.

As children, we depend on our parents and caregivers for protection and safety. Our survival depends on making sure we are secure with them. Our caregivers were responsible for modeling for us how to experience our emotions by creating a safe and nurturing relationship where we learned to express our feelings and feel validated. Perhaps a parent was emotionally distant while physically present; perhaps your emotions inconvenienced your parents; perhaps your parents criticized you and accused you of being weak and needy; perhaps your emotions made your caregivers feel angry with you; perhaps they would punish you and tell you to pull yourself together; or perhaps they were emotionally distanced from you, became disengaged, and neglected you. Perhaps your parents became angry or anxious when you expressed an emotion so you hid your feelings to make them less anxious or less angry in order to sustain the relationship. Either way, we learn to hide our feelings to make our caregivers feel comfortable; to avoid them hurting us, verbally or physically; or to avoid them abandoning us. We hide our emotional life to attach to a parent with whom we cannot share the truth.

How Do We Avoid Our Emotions?

The truth is, it is never our emotions that cause our issues but the ways we choose to avoid those emotions. We avoid feeling our feelings by choosing methods to distract and numb ourselves. These methods are defense mechanisms, what I call *cuckoo-coping companions*. Defense mechanisms are maladaptive ways we seek to protect ourselves from pain by avoiding our true feelings, such as a painful breakup or getting fired. Cuckoo-coping companions are ways we numb our pain through food, sex, drugs, alcohol, and social media, for example. Both methods are self-inflicted cuckoos because they are self-sabotaging behaviors and toxic thought patterns that keep us stuck. They are deeply ingrained habits that fend off anxiety when a painful emotion surfaces (see more on these methods in chapter 5, "What Feeds a Cuckoo?").

A common defense mechanism is intellectualizing, which means a person thinks rather than feels to avoid their current painful experience. Therefore, during a session a person provides a thought rather than a feeling. There is a distinction between one's thoughts and emotions and most people do not know the difference. When I ask my clients in cuckoo relationships how they feel, some of their responses include the following:

"I feel like my spouse doesn't understand me."

"I feel like leaving my job."

"I feel empty."

"I feel confused."

"I feel stuck."

These are all thoughts. Not one of them is a feeling.

It takes time to help my clients identify this defense of intellectualizing and feel their real emotions (anger, fear, sadness). For example, during a couple's session, one of them might say, "I feel like my spouse doesn't understand me." This is a statement of thought rather than an expression of emotion. The underlying emotion to the thought statement in this case was anger toward their spouse. Expressing anger in intimate relationships creates anxiety for this person due to past painful experiences where they learned that expressing anger leads to abandonment.

Another person was feeling stuck at work because their boss was treating them poorly. Rather than sharing how they felt toward their boss, they said, "I feel like leaving my job." This, too, is not a feeling; it is a thought. It is what they want to do, not how they feel. This person might believe they are being taken advantage of and feel anger toward their boss, but they are afraid to feel the anger and admit it to themselves or their boss because they are afraid it means they are weak or incapable, or they might lose their job if they express their true anger. They might also say, "I feel worried," which is also not a feeling but anxiety that is covering up a feeling. In reality, this person is angry at their boss for setting unrealistic expectations and threatening their job if all tasks are not completed. They might also respond "I feel stuck" or "I feel confused." Again, these are thoughts, not feelings. It is important to get in touch with the real emotion, and then the "what to do" knowledge, such as learning to set boundaries, will come.

Take a moment and ask yourself, "How do I feel toward the cuckoo in my life?" Distinguish between your thoughts and your feelings. How do you experience that feeling? In what ways have you been burying that feeling?

False Beliefs versus Truths: The Role of Emotion and Christian Spirituality

Another way people have learned to avoid their emotions, besides from their childhood experiences with their primary caregivers, is through false teachings from their church.

The following are false beliefs about the role of emotion and faith: emotions are not from God, emotions are sinful, emotions should be ignored, emotions are irrelevant to your spiritual life, emotions mean you lack trust in God, emotions thwart following the will of God, emotions equate to an inferior Christian life, emotions should not be addressed in a church setting, and emotions are an obstacle to faith and need to be disciplined or controlled.

The following are truths about emotion and faith: God created us in his image with emotions, God experiences us and speaks to us through emotion, emotion is a reflection of what God experiences in his heart, Scripture describes God's emotions, emotions are designed to be an intricate part of our faith journey, one of the Enemy's greatest tricks is to shut us down emotionally, and emotions play an essential role in the conviction of sin leading to repentance.

Emotions Are Indicators, Not Dictators

We are created in the image and likeness of God (Gen. 1:26). Our emotions are a natural part of who we are and how we were created. Again, emotions are nondebatable, biological realities that require close attention. If we deny, ignore, or numb our emotions with food or alcohol, we are dismissing vital data God intended for us when he created us. God speaks to us in many ways including through our emotions. Emotions keep us in the present moment rather than hiding from past hurts or anxiously anticipating the future. Emotions keep us honest and authentic.

Our emotions are indicators, not dictators, meaning that we do not let our emotions govern our behavior. We are not led by our emotions. We pay attention to them and the valuable information they provide us. Experiencing emotion is normal, not abnormal. They are part of what it means to be human. When we avoid our negative emotions, we have a tendency to avoid our positive emotions, too, such as joy. Selective emotional avoidance, however, is not possible because you become numb to feelings.

It is not possible to grow spiritually beyond your emotional immaturity.

There is a connection between your spiritual life and your emotional life, which means you cannot grow spiritually beyond where you are stuck emotionally. Our spiritual growth is significantly stunted when there is an absence of emotional growth.

When we ignore and disconnect from our emotional parts, we go through the motions of our faith in terms of prayers, spiritual disciplines, and ministry. Yet when we don't allow emotion to enter these experiences, we are unable to love God and our neighbor as ourselves wholeheartedly because we lack authenticity. If we cannot tell the truth about how we feel to ourselves, how can we tell it to other people? As humans we have an innate desire to be fully known and accepted for who we *really* are.

We can know Scripture intellectually but not experientially, personally, and intimately. Therefore we engage in Christian behaviors of doing yet live disconnected from our own hearts. God designed us in such a way that when our emotions are also involved in our spiritual experience, we deepen our intimacy with God. When the Spirit moves and speaks, we do not solely receive it intellectually, but we feel it deep within our hearts. Scripture says David was a man after God's own heart. The psalms are a beautiful example of David's embrace of a wide array of emotions such as joy, anger, fear, sadness, shame, and despair. He made mistakes. He repented. He obeyed. He grew and matured. He invited God into the depths of his heart. He was real.

The Emotions of God Found in Scripture

God is emotional. Throughout Scripture we see that God feels a plethora of emotions: compassion, joy, sadness, longing, jealousy, pleasure, mourning, love, laughter, and anger.

The following two scriptures reflect and describe the deeply intense emotions of Jesus and the Spirit:

> *And when Jesus went out He saw a great multitude;*
> *and He was moved with compassion for them,*
> *and healed their sick.* (MATT. 14:14)

"Moved with compassion" in this verse is the Greek word *splanchnizomai*: "To be moved with deep compassion or pity. The Greeks regarded the bowels (*splanchna*) as the place where strong and powerful emotions originated. The place where tender mercies and feelings of affection, compassion, sympathy, and pity originated. It is the direct motive for at least five of Jesus's miracles."[13]

The Spirit who dwells in us yearns jealously. (JAMES 4:5)

The Greek word for "yearn" is *epipotheo*, meaning "to long for, desire, to pursue with love, to lust."[14] Strong's Concordance defines lust as "to dote upon, intensely crave possession."

The word is used to describe the intense yearning the Spirit has for us. *Epipotheo* depicts a jealous love that is analogous to a partner boiling with anger. The Spirit is possessive of us. The picture is like that of a person who must have someone. That is how much God loves us. He is jealous of what takes our attention away from time with him. We often do not believe we have that much influence on God or that he experiences such intense emotions toward us.

The Shame Cuckoo

The emotion of shame, whether it be spiritual or relational, is toxic and creates unnecessary suffering. Many people feel stuck in unhealthy relationships, addictions, perfectionism, and people pleasing, and they have developed a mindset where they believe something is inherently wrong with them. Who they are equates to what they do or don't do. They do not realize they have a cuckoo in their life and its name is shame.

Shame is an intensely painful, self-conscious emotion during which we believe we are flawed, condemned, broken, and unworthy of love. Shame drives people to hide their transgressions from others, including God. When we are feeling shame, we are acutely aware of what is wrong with us. Rather than believing we are inherently flawed, it is important to become aware of the root of the shame, whether it be the presence of a self-inflicted cuckoo or a relationship cuckoo.

When we have a cuckoo in our life who is never satisfied, it leads to experiences of shame because we cannot please them regardless of how hard we try or how much we give of ourselves to make the relationship work. It is impossible to satisfy a cuckoo because they blame you and point out your flaws; they do not take responsibility for their harmful behavior, which, in their eyes, is always someone else's fault. Due to their deceptive and manipulative nature, we tend to believe their lies about us and we end up feeling worthless, unlovable, and wrong all the time. This shameful disillusionment leaves us wondering, *What is wrong with me?* instead of asking *What is not working in this relationship?*, or *Is this not reciprocal?*, or *Is this person harming me?*

Our self-inflicted cuckoos also provide opportunities for shame to manifest. Maybe the issue is not a person but rather your ministry or career that has gradually developed into an obsessive preoccupation that has taken over your life. Most days you feel ashamed to have neglected your marriage, children, friends, and health.

The Voice of Shame and the Voice of Conviction

On countless occasions, clients feel ashamed because they confuse conviction of sin as condemnation and shame rather than a call to repentance. This mostly stems from some false teachings in the church. This saddens my heart. My goal is to help my clients understand the truth about shame, especially lies they believe about conviction and repentance, which is a common theme in therapy.

The voice of shame when dealing with conviction of sin sounds like the following. A sense of dread, doubt, and fear comes over you. A paralyzing feeling of insecurity and inadequacy appears. You are abruptly reminded of your past failures and haunting memories of how you hurt others. A voice tells you, "You know that sin issue, that problem you are struggling with and can't seem to overcome? You should know better by now and have this perfectly sorted out. Until you fix it, Jesus is displeased with you and disappointed that you are *still* battling with this. Here is what you need to do: overcome this in your own strength because grace has run out at this point, and don't tell anyone about it until you stop doing it."

The voice of conviction in dealing with sin that leads to repentance sounds like the following. Imagine being enveloped in a warm blanket, Jesus gently approaching you, looking deeply into your eyes, smiling, putting his arms around you, and saying, "I love you so much. You are my precious child. I am so pleased with you right now, as you are, just for being you. You are incredibly special to me. I think about you every moment of every day. My heart aches for you as you wrestle with this. Don't be ashamed, dear one. I already know you have been struggling over this issue. You are not alone. I want to help you if you will allow me in. We have been through so much together, haven't we? I will not abandon you now. Will you trust me? I have something so beautiful to give you in place of this thing that you can't seem to let go. Will you release your grasp and give it up? I am willing when you are ready."

Conviction is rooted in love. Shame is rooted in fear.

The Spirit convicts (convinces) us of our identity as a child of God. The Holy Spirit abides within us, according to Jesus, as our helper who is always with us and reminding us of our righteousness in Christ Jesus. He wants to help us, not condemn us. He does not motivate us to repentance through guilt and condemnation

(Rom. 8:1). Guilt and condemnation do not lead to repentance; they lead to shame. Shame and guilt lead to self-hate and self-attack. Conviction leads to genuine healing, making amends, and repentance.

Spiritually speaking, Satan also represents the voice of shame who wants to have us identify with our sinful nature rather than our identity in Christ and therefore to hide ourselves as did Adam and Eve, naked and afraid. When we are in shame, we fall from a place of God, from consciousness to a place of self-consciousness.

Neither God nor Jesus nor the Holy Spirit will ever come to you and say, "This is what's wrong with you." Rather, they will gently suggest, "This is what is missing in your relationship with me, and I invite you to give this thing over to me so I can replace it with something beautiful, something better." Essentially, shame says *this is wrong* and conviction says *this is missing*.

> *God's kindness is intended to lead you to repentance.* (ROM. 2:4 NIV)

The Greek word for "kindness" is *chrestotes*: "Goodness in action, sweetness of disposition, gentleness in dealing with others, kindness, affability."[15]

For this reason, repentance is meant to be a joyful experience, because we learn to trust in God's goodness. This is not easy, yet repentance is helpful, productive, and adaptive—it leads to growth and transformation. We begin to recognize how our obedience to Christ provides incredible blessing, and we walk away in a better place.

My Conviction Story

I began watching a television series highly recommended by a friend. Immediately I was hooked. The series became a distraction, a cuckoo. As the riveting plot unfolded with each episode, I found myself preoccupied with the show even when I was not watching it. Slowly and subtly my thought life and emotional energy were consumed. From the moment I got home from work until I went to sleep, I spent the entire evening watching this series.

I started to feel embarrassed that I was neglecting other things and people who had brought me joy in the evenings. I felt ashamed that perfectionism was rearing its ugly head. The voice of shame whispered, *What's wrong with you? You are a professional counselor, and you can't stop watching a silly show?* Although I was tempted to believe those lies, I chose to listen to the voice of the Holy Spirit and invited him into the situation and asked him to convict me of what was missing. It felt awkward and vulnerable at first.

I focused my attention from what was wrong with me to what was missing in my relationship with Jesus, others, and even myself. Ever since I was a little girl, I had a vivid imagination and a highly active and creative thought life, which have served me well as an adult, both personally and professionally. I also find joy in daily life in simple pleasures. I talk to Jesus all day long about everything; it's an intimacy I have come to cherish.

My moment of conviction came quite suddenly and unexpectedly. In that moment I felt this warm, loving presence surround me, and I had this thought: *What did I used to think about?* I felt sad. All my thoughts, creativity, and imaginations had been overtaken by this show, and I realized I missed having my own thoughts and letting my mind wander freely and creatively. That is how I process my inner world void of distractions. I had been tormenting myself with shame and trying to stop watching the show instead of focusing on what was missing in my life. Some people might think, *What's the big deal? It's just a show! So what if you just thought about it too much.*

For me, it became a distraction. The reality was I felt disconnected from my own thoughts and feelings because I was spending my evenings absorbed in the characters' emotions and feelings, partly because my joy comes from intuiting and sharing the emotional experiences of those around me as well as learning why people do the things they do. But these weren't real relationships, and they were taking up more space in my life than real people were. I missed those people.

The shame cuckoo can rear its ugly head whether it is a distraction that becomes a bit obsessive or a debilitating emotion that creates immense pain.

Are you suffering under the heavy weight of the shame cuckoo? I encourage you to read aloud to yourself the voice of conviction statements above and then ask God, *What is missing in my life and in my relationship with you? What beautiful thing do you want to give me in place of this* [fill in the blank] *that I can't seem to let go of?*

Feeling Our Feelings Helps Us Face Our Cuckoos

Each of our emotions serves a purpose and points us back to our true selves. What a powerful gift that God created us with emotions. When we share our feelings, we share the truth of our experience in that moment. When we do not know how we feel, we are not aware of our boundaries, needs, wants, and desires, and we allow our cuckoo's needs and wants to consume our own. When we fear our feelings, we simultaneously fear our cuckoos because we don't want to be judged, criticized, rejected, blamed, or shamed. Yet we lack the wisdom our emotions provide. Emotional pain helps us avoid or leave hurtful and abusive relationships and situations where a cuckoo is present. When dealt with appropriately, feeling our feelings empowers us to know ourselves and who we are in Christ, void of shame, so we can face our cuckoos confidently.

I use the following letter template in my practice to help my clients get in touch with the feelings they are experiencing because of being in a relationship with a cuckoo. Please write out on a separate sheet of paper and use the below questions as your guide:

Dear [name the cuckoo who has hurt or harmed you],

The purpose of this letter is to share with you the pain I received because of [write down specifically what they did or said that was painful for you]:

_____

_____

As a result of this behavior, I want to share with you how I truly feel:

_____

_____

The effects of the pain I have experienced in our relationship has brought hurt to my life in these ways:

_____

_____

My needs, wants, and desires are the following:

_____

_____

My boundaries for the future include:

_____

_____

Here are the things I love and appreciate about you:

_____

_____

Note that this letter is intended for your healing. You do not have to give this letter to your cuckoo. The purpose is for you to express your feelings by writing them down.

You may also invite Jesus into the experience by praying and making a choice to forgive this person. Forgiveness does not equate to allowing the toxic behaviors to continue or release your cuckoo from taking responsibility for their actions. Forgiveness is a way to release yourself from harboring unresolved pain and anger buried deep within your heart. Unforgiveness can zap your energy, steal your joy, and take a tremendous toll on your body and can lead to grudges, bitterness, and resentment. These can become toxic to your overall health, and they hold the potential to block your emotional and physical healing and God's healing power.

Our emotional health is as important as our mental and physical health. Gaining an awareness and understanding of our emotions by facing our feelings and learning from them instead of fearing them is the true path to healing and the first step to doing something about it. Identifying the root cause of your issues can help you break free so you have more control of your life rather than allowing the cuckoo to control you, making you suffer as a result. An abundant, joyful, meaningful, and more peaceful life awaits you.

Here are some helpful truths to remember:

I don't need to fear and fight my feelings. They will provide me with valuable information.

Emotions are uncomfortable, not dangerous, sinful, or wrong.

I am experiencing feelings that are painful and I am not to blame for them.

My feelings can be channeled into healthy actions that will help me and not hurt me.

Facing my cuckoo may seem impossible right now, but I must avoid being helpless and move forward with courage.

I have more control over my emotions than I realize. They will not overwhelm me, and I can choose to feel them.

My feelings are indicators, not dictators.

I can turn these feelings of being hurt by my cuckoo into my allies rather than my enemies. They can help me find the solution I've been searching for.

I will allow my feelings to provide clarity on what is causing my symptoms and suffering.

This, too, shall pass.

CHAPTER 4

THE CUCKOO OF LOSS

The Paradox of Grief

No one ever told me that grief felt so like fear.
—C. S. LEWIS

W E ALL EXPERIENCE LOSS. ANOTHER COMMON EMOTION we bury is sadness in the form of grief. Grief is a deep sadness and reality-based emotional reaction to loss. When we avoid our grief, it becomes a cuckoo in our life by bringing additional suffering to an already painful loss and eventually steals our joy.

With my clients, I have found that grief is the most debilitating and painful emotion and therefore the most feared and avoided. This is understandably so.

A few times each week I spend my break between clients in my childhood neighborhood, which is less than a mile from my private practice. No matter what changes I go through, good or bad, this neighborhood is always there. It never changes, and this brings comfort. Not that my childhood was all wonderful; it wasn't. In fact, it was quite painful and traumatic at times. As I sit on the bench across the street from the house where I grew up, my home until I was fifteen years old, I think to myself that Charles Dickens said it best: *It was the best of times, it was the worst of times.*

I consistently sought refuge by being outdoors, running through the woods, playing in the creek, riding my bike, creating forts, and catching fireflies. When I wasn't spending time with friends, I spent much of my early years alone with my imagination, which was lit up in my own inner world.

Now I walk the sidewalks of my childhood neighborhood and long for something I can't quite identify or articulate. There is a deep sense of desire, an ache. The seasons of my life come and go despite my yearning for time to stand still in this moment, yet I know in my heart I cannot stay. This is no longer my home.

When I was growing up, my grandmother (Ga-Ga) lived across the street from my house. She was my safe place throughout my childhood and early teenage years before she passed away when I was sixteen years old. They say nobody is perfect, but *she* was. I still have a handwritten note she left on my dresser one morning: "You are the very best of everything." When my home life became unsafe, I sought refuge at her house and often stayed the night. We had a familiar routine, and I cherished every minute we spent together. After bath time I would change into one of her nightgowns, instead of the pajamas I had packed, because they smelled like her. I would act silly and prance around the house; she never cared what mood I was in. I could always be myself. It was just me, no parents or siblings to interfere during our special times.

I would lie next to her each night after I had my sugar cookies and milk, and she would run her fingers through my hair for hours until I fell asleep. For years she sat in the same spot on her sofa, every afternoon, watching television while I was outside rollerblading, skateboarding, riding my bike, and playing with friends. It gave me such comfort and security to know she was right across the street.

Ga-Ga was diagnosed with liver cancer and her health deteriorated rapidly. One afternoon as I was preparing to leave for cheerleading practice, I stopped by to see her and had a feeling it would be the last time. As I looked at her in the hospice bed while I stood in the doorway, I debated staying and not going to practice, telling her how much I loved her and sitting beside her. I left instead. She died that evening, only three months after her diagnosis. She was only in her seventies. I bottled up my pain while others were grieving around me. I was numb. I sat with my family at her funeral and wondered why I couldn't shed a single tear.

It was one of those traumas that left a very deep mark on me.

Something died inside of me.

Unknown to me, on the day I left for cheerleading practice, I had flipped the switch to Off. That switch was my emotions.

Sadness. Pain. Fear. Anger. It was easier to live in denial and bury my pain.

Soon after, intense guilt crept in, and for years I was haunted by the memory of not having had a last goodbye with her.

I was not able to put a voice to my grief. Therefore, it did not go away. For years I lost myself. That carefree, imaginative, creative little girl with the pigtails who could live joyfully outside her circumstances was gone.

Scripture reveals a powerful truth about joy and sadness; they have a connection.

Those who sow in tears shall reap in joy. (Ps. 126:5)

Weeping may endure for a night, but joy
comes in the morning. (Ps. 30:5)

For I will turn their mourning to joy, will comfort them,
and make them rejoice rather than sorrow. (Jer. 31:13)

I never allowed myself to cry, so I never reaped joy. The cuckoo of my unresolved grief grew larger and larger as the years passed. I did not notice it for almost a decade, but the sadness did not leave; it was buried and slowly eroded my joy over time. After my grandmother passed, my family would gather in our living room and watch old videos of Ga-Ga while they cried and laughed as they relived the memories we shared with her. I would leave the room immediately before they pressed Play. I thwarted my own process of healing, and I never knew God as comforter in my grandmother's death. I had mastered the art of cutting off my feelings in earlier pain I had experienced as a child.

Grief and Abuse

Before our present grief experience, we learn very early, as children, to cut off our emotional pain and anger when abuse takes place. This is a survival and coping mechanism. When you are told you are at fault, it is not safe to feel and express the pain inflicted by abuse. That is what abuse does to a person; it causes shame. You learn to analyze your abuser instead of feeling your pain. That's an attempt to prevent the abuse from happening again, even though the abuser is unpredictable. This is why grieving our present losses is so important; it can connect us to past unresolved pain and shame to bring healing to those wounds.

Being in an abusive relationship with a cuckoo creates an environment of shame and fear. Because the cuckoo deceives and manipulates, we often question our reality as they blame us for things that are not our fault. They also make excuses for hurting us. Even if their current relationship with their cuckoo is not abusive, many of my clients still experience grief in relationships with a cuckoo. This is because, at a deep level, they have lost themselves by taking care of the cuckoo who consumes all their time and energy, thus chronically neglecting their own needs and wants. The cuckoo relationship dynamic is costly as they lose their own heart's desires, hopes, and dreams while they are being smothered by the crushing weight of the cuckoo.

The Outcome of Unresolved Grief

Loss, however, is as normal as breathing when we avoid our feelings of sadness or do not go through the grieving process. Sufferings such as anxiety and depression are common outcomes. In addition to creating suffering, unresolved grief sabotages joy. It is not possible to selectively numb our emotions, because when we numb painful emotions, we numb the positive emotions too.

When we do not embrace the grieving process, we lose our joy. For this reason, joy entails vulnerability because we must risk and develop courage to face our sadness.

Due to their unresolved grief, my clients live in fear of being hurt again, which drives them to take back control and self-protect by closing their hearts to everyone surrounding them. This defense mechanism prevents them from experiencing truly rewarding and intimate relationships with others.

I've discovered that avoiding the grieving process becomes the undercurrent of much pain being manifested in unhealthy relationships, sabotaging behaviors, and addictions. The outcome of not experiencing your grief can become a self-inflicted cuckoo. Grief is not an isolated emotion; it carries with it a wide array of pain, such as sadness, guilt, fear, anger, and doubt. Suppressed pain does not disappear. It only grows deeper, and we become vulnerable to developing ways to numb our pain to cope.

At times, avoiding emotional pain can manifest in physical pain within our bodies because at a deep-seated level it can seem easier to locate and feel physical pain rather than complex emotional pain. I have witnessed countless ways my clients avoid grief, but the emotional pain eventually manifests in their bodies as chronic fatigue, migraines, back pain, muscle tension, insomnia, and other unexplained medical symptoms that no doctor can diagnose with a physical cause.

Confusing Grief

Sometimes we are unexpectedly hit with grief upon making positive decisions, such as ending an unhealthy relationship, leaving a job that no longer brought fulfillment, or moving to a new place we are excited about. Confusion sets in because we are sad about something seemingly progressive and optimistic. We might think to ourselves, *Did I make a mistake? If this is something I wanted to do, why am I so sad?* We might begin to doubt ourselves and even God. *Am I crazy? Did I not hear God correctly?*

We grieve when we lose, even if the loss is a good thing. By facing the reality of our loss, we can grieve what has passed and embrace what we have.

There is a process connected with grief, because losing someone or something is not an occasion or an event. And it does not happen just once. It whispers to us in unexpected ways and moments that take us off guard. Allow those waves of sorrow to wash over you and be certain that joy is near and will lift you back up again.

Sadness to Joy

> The LORD *is close to the brokenhearted and saves* *those who are crushed in spirit.* (Ps. 34:18 NIV)

In my case, nearly a decade after Ga-Ga's passing, I unexpectedly found her purse in my mother's closet. It had remained untouched since the last time she used it. The purse still smelled like her. I made the life-changing decision to open it and pull out each item. I was surprised by the number of tears that poured out with each memory. I allowed the waves of sorrow to wash over me. The toothpicks, her red lipstick, her Juicy Fruit gum, the lollipops from the bank, her perfume, a prescription bottle, and grocery lists.

It was as if someone flipped the switch to On after having been off for so long. Much to my surprise, I felt relief. I experienced God's presence, comforting me like a warm blanket. It wasn't too late after all. In fact, I was right on time. The intense pain of years of unresolved grief flooded back to me, and God used that moment to bring healing. The good news was, although my joy was missing for years, I have a redemptive and powerful God who was able to restore my joy and who now allows me to help others on their journey of grieving.

Now, in my mind's eye, I can see Ga-Ga with her glasses hanging around her neck, her bright red lipstick, and her beautiful smile. There was such warmth to her. Her presence brought peace and assurance that everything was OK.

As I share this memory now, my heart still aches to recall it. Before Ga-Ga's passing, I had never known anyone who had died, and it never occurred to me that someday my grandmother would no longer be a vital part of my everyday life. The greatest gift a person can give you is to show you are loved no matter what, you have a safe place you can call home, and you can be yourself without fear of judgment.

Ga-Ga modeled for me the heart of Jesus and what a relationship with him can be like. I do not have my Ga-Ga anymore, but I do have and will always have her memory and an experience of Jesus as my shelter, strong tower, and very present help in time of need (Ps. 46:1).

Grief Is Part of Your Story

Throughout my clinical career, I have learned a powerful and validating truth about grief after meeting with countless clients who came to me presenting secondary symptoms of depression and anxiety, a feeling of being stuck and finding no relief from medication. Because of my own struggles with grieving, rather than solely focusing on my clients' specific symptoms of anxiety and depression, I now ask them to share with me the story of their loss. The loss might be of a family member, a relationship, a job, a home, a dream of marriage or children or a career that never happened for them, or an ongoing relationship with a significant other who has left emotionally while still being physically present.

Healing occurs when my clients feel they have permission to not expend any more emotional energy trying to figure out why they are still grieving or why they are not strong enough to move on. As I mentioned earlier, choosing to grieve in the first place is the most powerful step. Grief is cyclical, and the pain can manifest itself in different ways that can bring confusion if you do not realize grief consists of multiple layers that involve healing. Grief is neither linear nor a black-and-white experience.

Grief is about giving yourself permission to experience the loss in the moment you feel it and not to rationalize it away, not to try to be strong or beat yourself up. "I should be over this by now." "What's wrong with me?" It has taken me quite some time to realize, softly and simply, those moments are not a time for self-diagnosis; there is nothing wrong with you.

The loss of my grandmother is part of my story to preserve and to embrace, not a shameful event to hide in the past. It is part of who I am, and it always will be.

Happiness Is Situational, Joy Is Relational

Happiness is situational because it is dependent on our circumstances. Happiness is externally focused. Joy is an internal state of being that is not dependent on our circumstances. I define joy as a deep-seated place of abiding in our hearts and souls. Being joyful does not mean you are always happy; we can have joy during painful situations, such as loss. Happiness is fleeting, and joy flourishes not only when things are good but also in difficult times.

Joy is rooted in our faith in God, who is bigger than our circumstances. The beautiful part about joy is that we do not have to bring it about in our strength. Joy is dependent on our relationship with God, and he is full of compassion and comfort. A prevalent Greek word for "joy" in the New Testament is *chara*. *Chara* means "joy, calm delight, or inner gladness." The word is also connected to *chairo*, which means "to rejoice," and *charis*, which means "grace." True joy comes from our relationship with God and relying on his grace to help us overcome painful trials. We can express our grief and pour our hearts out to God when we experience pain.

Choosing joy means choosing to embrace grief. As stated in the Scripture passage at the beginning of the chapter, those who sow in tears shall reap in joy. God promises to turn our mourning to joy and to comfort us. Mourning consists of feelings, and being comforted requires something we need comfort from, our pain. Pain is an inevitable reality of loss, and joy is an inevitable reality of grief.

The Paradox of Grief

The paradox of grief is that it brings joy. It restores our hearts and brings healing to our souls. Grieving is necessary; it is good and cleansing. The lie we believe is that grief will leave us in despair, so we fear it rather than embrace it. Grief can feel unwelcomed, unexpected, and inconvenient. But I invite you to make the choice to grieve and allow the waves of sadness to roll over you.

These realities about grief can either frighten you or free you. I invite you to surrender your feelings of fear, dread, and doubt and replace them with the hope and joy that will come.

Your life is a masterpiece.

Grief is just one piece put in place precisely by God.

CHAPTER 5

WHAT FEEDS A CUCKOO?

Lies We Believe and Defenses We Use

Truth is like the sun. You can shut it out
for a time, but it ain't goin' away.
—ELVIS PRESLEY

THIS CHAPTER REVEALS WHAT FEEDS A CUCKOO AND THE corresponding patterns that keep us stuck in a continuous cycle of suffering. These are avoiding pain and the truth it contains, believing lies that hold us captive, and establishing defenses and coping mechanisms to protect us. You will learn to embrace the deepest truths of who you are, who others are, and who God is so you can be healed.

The Distinction Between Pain and Suffering

My work centers on this truth: just because you experience pain does not mean you have to suffer.

Everyone who seeks healing has a painful story. Life is painful. It's hard. It's scary. It's full of disappointment. I've discovered the following pattern in my work with clients: people are afraid to face their pain as truth, as reality, because they do not know how to deal with it. Therefore, many people do not understand their own suffering. They are unaware of the cuckoos that are right in front of them. I help people turn toward their pain instead of avoiding it so they will face the truth as reality and they can be free and live a meaningful life.

Pain consists of what we experience, emotionally and physically, in relation to a distressing situation or life event, such as losing a job or getting divorced. We all experience pain throughout our life: failure, heartbreak, illness, loss, rejection, abandonment. Your pain started before your suffering did. Suffering, however, is an indication that you have a cuckoo in your life.

Suffering comes in various forms: anxiety, depression, shame, regret, addiction, guilt, chronic stress, sleep issues, perfectionism, hopelessness, low self-esteem. Suffering consists of the ways we avoid facing our cuckoos and their corresponding pain. Suffering consists of the lies we tell ourselves about our pain and the defense and coping mechanisms we use to protect ourselves from our pain.

Each of us has a cuckoo in our life at some point, whether it be an unhealthy relationship or a self-sabotaging behavior (a self-inflicted cuckoo). Although cuckoos exist and try to invade our lives with their devious disguises, we do not have to be their host, and we can make choices to stop feeding them.

Suffering occurs when the cuckoo behaviors and relationships continue and take over your life. Cuckoos become your purpose because their eggs hatch instead of your own. You are left empty, confused, anxious, depressed, unfilled, and exhausted. You suffer. As a result, your true self and your identity are consumed by your cuckoo.

Knowing who you are and what you really want can be difficult when you live with a cuckoo. Cuckoos produce self-doubt by constantly lying to you and manipulating you. You are slowly deceived out of trusting yourself: your reality, your intuition, your thoughts, your feelings. Your true self is buried beneath the toxic weight of the cuckoo.

Your Pain Contains Truth, and Truth Dispels Cuckoos

We suffer when we avoid truth. But our pain contains truth, namely, the truth of who we are, who others are, and who God is.

First and foremost, truth is factual; truth consists of all the things we cannot inevitably control about our life: getting older, getting sick, our annoying in-laws, losing our job, our spouse having an affair. We cannot change the reality of our circumstance; we can only change ourselves. Truth is synonymous with reality, which is "the true situation that exists . . . something that actually happens: a real event, occurrence, or situation."[16] You cannot change facts (painful circumstances), but you can address, change, and heal the ways you deny those facts through toxic thinking patterns, avoiding painful emotions, and the destructive ways you cope and protect yourself. Neither can you control your past traumas, memories of failure, rejections, abandonments, or humiliating experiences, yet you can defuse their powerful ability to continue to hurt you, create fear, and control you.

Biblically speaking, the written Word of God is truth. Jesus said of himself "I am … the truth" (John 14:6). The Greek word for "truth" in John 17:17 is *aletheia*, meaning "of a truth, in reality, in fact, certainly."[17] The Bible also points to truth as reality: "Those who worship Him must worship in spirit and truth [reality]" (John 4:24 AMP). In my practice I've discovered that so many people are frustrated, confused, and lost with regard to their faith and feeling unable to hear God's voice and receive guidance or comfort from him during challenging times. This is primarily because they are running away from their pain and denying the reality of their present circumstances, and by doing so they are running toward ways to numb their pain, which blocks out truth. God, however, operates in truth.

As discussed in chapter 3, "The Cuckoo of Not Feeling Your Feelings," we are created in the image of God with emotions that are a biological reality that occur automatically in our brain and body. Emotions are a large part of who we are, and they are important. Denying and avoiding our painful emotions robs us of experiencing truth because we are disconnecting from a real part of how we are wired, allowing us to be susceptible to believing lies. Lies become the cornerstone of our minds, corrupting our thought life and producing distorted beliefs not grounded in reality or rooted in truth.

Our emotions are indicators, not dictators, which means we do not let our emotions govern our behavior. We pay attention to them and the valuable information God intended them to provide. A wounded heart filled with fear, shame, and unresolved pain will seek to protect rather than allow God as our protector to lead us into his truth.

When the truth is revealed, the healing process can begin. Often the truth is hiding beneath our pain, covered up by the lies we tell ourselves, the lies of the Enemy, and the lies of our cuckoo. Truth is the catalyst for healing, yet it is not always easy to face. Many people run from their pain rather than embrace it, and understandably so, because it takes vulnerability, strength, and courage to face it. We've all heard that the truth will set you free, but it will make you angry first! Facing our pain means facing our scary feelings and our fears, and facing the possibility of rejection and abandonment, grief, sadness, and heartache.

The way to freedom is to face your pain and seek to understand it, feel it, listen to its message, and learn from it and the truth it contains. When you continually run away from the reality of difficult circumstances and relationships, you run the risk of prolonging your healing and creating additional layers of suffering.

By running away from our pain, we are running toward ways to numb our pain. The need to avoid pain is part of our human nature. But healing and transformation can begin when we face our cuckoos. By continuing to feed our cuckoos and taking care of them constantly, we become disillusioned because we are not in touch with reality and become vulnerable to more cuckoos.

Cuckoos steal, manipulate, lie, strip us of our identity, and become our purpose. We spend our whole life managing our cuckoos instead of living a fulfilled life. Facing the truth in our lives not only reveals who or what causes us to suffer, but it also gives us the courage to face our cuckoos and face the pain that contains truth.

Truth dispels cuckoos.

Strongholds: Self-Erected Prisons That Keep Pain in and Truth Out

How do we avoid pain and thus block the truth it contains? By erecting strongholds to protect ourselves. Strongholds offer a false sense of protection from pain, and not until we understand this will we recognize we've been protecting our cuckoos and actively taking care of them.

What is a stronghold? Psychologically speaking, I describe a stronghold as a mental fortress established to protect us from an outside attack, that is, anything we perceive as threatening or dangerous. A stronghold is used to defend a particular personal belief against outside opposition from an enemy. But when we erect these mental fortresses, we become our own worst enemy because we are the prisoners within the fortress we have built around ourselves. Strongholds are essentially a personal bondage initially established in our mind and fortified thought by thought, just as a physical structure is built brick by brick. Behind every thought is a lie that we have been led to believe is true; therefore, we fight to protect the lies, causing us to reinforce the lies and keeping us stuck in a cycle of unnecessary suffering.

We are unaware that our strongholds are not protecting and helping us but rather harming us. The root issue behind strongholds is our unresolved pain and our unmet needs, which try to keep further pain out while keeping other pains in. We all have relational wounds, unmet needs, rejections, abandonments, traumatic memories, and shameful experiences that are very painful and difficult to face. Strongholds preserve these pains and prevent us from receiving truth, healing, and closeness with others.

Being in a relationship with a cuckoo is a lopsided relationship because we are chronically neglecting our self and our needs. Therefore, we become afraid and easily offended and isolate ourselves, believing all sorts of lies. We end up defending those lies to ourselves and to others who are trying to help, but we view their help as an attack, a threat.

Think of strongholds as a bird cage with a bunch of cuckoos flying around you, and you're the only one who can open the door. Strongholds keep your cuckoos in, and they are built with the hope of keeping pain out, but these strongholds actually prevent truth from coming in: the truth of who you really are, who your cuckoos are, and who God is. You are strong without your strongholds because knowing the truth is what sets you free. Strongholds keep you in a prison of paralyzing fear and create suffering. Strongholds attempt to protect your unmet needs and heal your wounds, but they really do the opposite.

Strongholds: Defense Mechanisms + Cuckoo-Coping Companions
Lies We Believe = Falsely Protect Us from Pain and Keep Out Truth

The apostle Paul described these strongholds: "For the weapons of our warfare are not carnal but mighty in God for pulling down strongholds, casting down arguments and every high thing that exalts itself against the knowledge of God, bringing every thought into captivity to the obedience of Christ" (2 Cor. 10:4–5). There is a connection between "pulling down strongholds" and taking "every thought into captivity." Strongholds are initially established in your mind, which is why it is important to take every thought captive.

Take your thoughts captive by frequently asking yourself, "Am I thinking about what I am thinking about?" "Is this thought helpful or harmful?" If you are having difficulty identifying if you are having a toxic thought, ask yourself, "How does this thought make me feel?" Perhaps you feel anxious, sad, or afraid. Experience your emotions, because they will help guide you into identifying what lie you are believing about yourself. For example, you feel sad about a recent breakup, and you believe you aren't good enough and you fear you will always be single and alone. Because of that false belief, you compromise your values and end up in another unhealthy relationship with a different cuckoo and the cycle repeats itself.

Each of these strongholds' components is discussed in greater detail in the following sections, and they cover the lies we believe and the specific defense mechanisms and coping companions. Strongholds are used to block out pain and truth, but the good news is that strongholds can be dismantled. Just as we build them up, we can tear them down. The first step is knowing the truth that you have erected a stronghold in your life. Tearing down a stronghold is a process because the stronghold was not built over-night. Like any structure or fortress, it was built brick by brick, thought by thought, and so it must come down brick by brick, thought by thought. This is not an easy endeavor. It takes courage, perseverance, and help from safe people as well as exposing our pain to God in order to be able to open the door to receive his truth and release our cuckoos.

Exposing the Lies You Believe So the Truth Can Set You Free

As mentioned in the previous section, behind every stronghold is a lie. Lies become toxic thinking patterns and false narratives we believe to be true. When we are told repeatedly that we are a failure, stupid, ugly, worthless, and unlovable, eventually we will start to believe these lies, which override the truth and lead to self-deception, self-doubt, and self-hatred. We suffer because we believe, at our core, that we are unsuccessful, unintelligent, unwanted, unloved, and unworthy. This filters the way we behave in our relationships, and we attract cuckoos.

Another way of understanding truth is to look at the cuckoo's falsehoods, its lies. Before the truth can set you free, it is important to identify the lies that are holding you captive. Just because a thought enters your mind does not mean it is true.

Because cuckoos are imposters by nature, crafty deceivers, they constantly lie to us through manipulative tactics aimed at having you question your own reality, thus making it difficult to distinguish what is true and what is a lie. Biblically speaking, lies represent the nature of the Enemy: "He was a murderer from the beginning, and does not stand in the truth, because there is no truth in him. When he speaks a lie, he speaks from his own resources, for he is a liar and the father of it" (John 8:44). Satan can lie to us, our cuckoos can lie to us, and we can lie to ourselves through false narratives.

Lies generate false narratives we create to cope with our pain. Essentially, we unconsciously and even instinctively tell ourselves stories about other people and our circumstances. As humans, we are meaning-making machines, which is how we make sense of our world and the people in it. We make meaning about the difficult situations or relationships in our lives and hope to make things easier and less hurtful. This dynamic creates unnecessary suffering. A false narrative is our interpretation or story based on the lies we believe and tell ourselves about our pain and what we make it mean rather than accepting it and dealing with it as it really is. Essentially, we are lying to ourselves through our thoughts, beliefs, judgments, and accusations. This method of coping through difficult times creates tremendous suffering.

In couple's counseling, it is common during a conflict for each person to fight the other's stories (the false narratives they have created about one another) rather than discuss what is really happening or how they are really feeling. Depending on the hurtful behavior or conflict they are currently experiencing, they have made meaning out of the present situation. He/she does not love me, accept me, cherish me, pursue me, need me, desire me, care about me.

Perhaps your spouse has been playing more golf or taking more yoga classes than normal. From a place of feeling rejected, you create a story that they are avoiding you purposely and not wanting to spend time with you. Rather than sharing this feeling because it might feel scary and vulnerable, you are afraid of being viewed as needy because you heard from a friend that a couple recently separated because someone was too needy and controlling. So you criticize your partner for not being there for you and accuse them of not caring about the relationship. In response, they anxiously scramble to defend themselves, accusing you of not appreciating them. This is a vicious cycle. The truth is the person is simply enjoying a hobby and needing a break from life stressors. Accusing, blaming, and criticizing does not give your partner a chance to speak to how you are really feeling and to come up with a solution, such as to go on date nights more often. Perhaps, throughout your childhood, one parent abandoned you and broke promises about spending time with you. Therefore, you are making meaning out of something that is not actually happening in your current relationship, yet you are suffering nonetheless.

If a spouse cheats, the person might tell themselves a lie, a story that it is all their fault, that they are unworthy of love, they will never get over this, or they will always be alone. The reality is, their spouse cheated. They are creating meaning out of the fact that their spouse cheated by creating a false narrative that it is their fault. They are believing lies that they will never be OK and will always be alone. They are avoiding their pain (anger, sadness, shame) because it is so scary. Perhaps they use alcohol or work to avoid their pain, which leads to other suffering, such as anxiety and depression, rather than work through the painful emotions that come with betrayal.

Another common pattern is the lie they tell themselves that, when something is hard, they make it mean something is wrong. Therefore, they try to fix what is wrong instead of facing what is hard. Most often they experienced childhood pain or trauma from their caregivers and felt shame that it was their fault, hence pain equates to shame, which becomes a foundational false belief into adulthood. When a client is avoiding the painful emotions of a hard situation or relationship because they believe the lie that they did something wrong, they suffer by obsessively operating in fix-it mode and end up in an isolated, confused, anxious bubble of toxic overthinking. (We will explore this cuckoo-making dynamic in chapter 8, "When You Become a Cuckoo: Making Yourself a Project to Fix.")

Intellectual Knowing or Relational Knowing?

Lies block us from experiencing the truth that leads to freedom: "You shall know the truth, and the truth shall make you free" (John 8:32). According to this Scripture, it is not only the truth that sets you free but also knowing the truth. The original Greek word for "know" is *ginosko*, which means to know truth through personal, firsthand experience.[18] Experience turns truth into a reality we know firsthand as opposed to head knowledge, knowledge gained intellectually. Knowledge in and of itself does not bring freedom, just as awareness does not lead to instant healing transformation.

Many clients have come to me for counseling after reading numerous self-help books and listening to podcasts on toxic people, addiction, perfectionism, anxiety, codependency, and dysfunctional relationships. Perhaps they have found some relief, yet they continue to remain stuck. Why? Because freedom and breakthrough come through personal experience. The first step is knowing through acquiring knowledge. The second step is knowing personally through experience. "[That you may really come] to know [practically, through experience for yourselves] the love of Christ, which far surpasses mere knowledge [without experience]" (Eph. 3:19 AMPC).

This means we need to experience our pain and embrace the reality of our circumstances, even if they're hard and scary. Likewise, we must feel our feelings and share our experiences with a safe person who knows us and can speak truth and help us to expose the lies we are believing to be true.

Learning to recognize the lies we believe and face the truth of our situations and relationships allows us to stop saying yes to our cuckoo's insatiable demands, whether our cuckoo is something we believe or someone lying to us, and to stop feeding them and carrying their load and doing their work instead of our own. Demolishing our strongholds will allow the truth in, the truth that sets us free.

Cuckoos Invade Our Lives and Our Defenses Rise

In addition to the lies we believe, we create defense mechanisms to distract ourselves from facing the reality of our difficult circumstances, such as a painful breakup, the loss of a dream or a loved one, or getting fired from work. Both lies and defense mechanisms are what we use to establish strongholds. This section will show you what defense mechanisms are and which specific ones you use.

I've found in my work with clients that their defense mechanisms are unconscious yet destructive ways they seek to protect themselves from pain by avoiding their true feelings. Defense mechanisms are self-sabotaging patterns of thinking and behaving that keep us stuck in a perpetual cycle of unnecessary suffering.

Just as we all have cuckoos in our life, we all use defense mechanisms. Defense mechanisms are the specific ways we lie to ourselves to avoid the reality of painful situations and our corresponding feelings, such as fear, sadness, anger, and grief. Defense mechanisms block truth, but knowing the truth is what sets us free from living in cuckoo land, stuck and miserable.

There are various forms of defense mechanisms. They include intellectualizing, isolating, people pleasing, rationalizing, minimizing, spiritualizing, performing, denying, playing the victim, projectizing, and fantasizing.

Intellectualizing: Reasoning, analyzing, and thinking about a problem to avoid feeling painful or uncomfortable emotions. Essentially, using a thought rather than a feeling.

This defense was discussed in chapter 3, "The Cuckoo of Not Feeling Your Feelings." There is a distinction between one's thoughts and one's emotions, but most people do not know the difference. When I ask my clients how they feel, these are some of their responses:

"I feel like my spouse doesn't understand me."

"I feel like leaving my job."

"I feel confused."

"I feel stuck."

As we noted before, the above responses are all thoughts. Not one of them is a feeling. The underlying emotions could be:

"I feel anger toward my spouse."

"I feel fearful that I will never find a fulfilling career."

"I feel sad that I am single and don't know why I can't find love."

It takes time to help my clients identify this defense of intellectualizing and feel their real emotions, such as anger, fear, or sadness.

Isolating: Detaching emotionally and physically withdrawing from others and refusing to be vulnerable.

People pleasing: Needing the approval of others and seeking to make them happy at the expense of placing another person's needs and desires above our own to avoid judgment, rejection, and abandonment.

Rationalizing: Explaining a reason to justify our behavior as opposed to describing the feeling.

Minimizing: Reducing and undervaluing the severity of feelings and their emotional significance. For example, "It's not that bad" or "It could be worse" (comparing one's situation to another's) or "It's not a big deal."

Spiritualizing: Using one's faith as an excuse to avoid painful emotions. For example, "I should be grateful to God for where I am" or "He is teaching me a lesson" or "My relationship with God is not secure" or "My faith must not be strong enough." Essentially, we are not being real with God, others, or ourselves about the pain we are truly experiencing.

Performing: Seeking worth and value through our accomplishments. Performing is avoiding painful emotions via work, busyness, or perfectionism.

Denying: Ignoring reality and pretending that painful emotions do not exist. "Nothing is wrong" or "I feel fine."

For example, let's say you and a close friend have been growing apart over the last couple of years, and instead of accepting the reality that your friend no longer responds to your invitations to spend time together, you continue to make significant efforts to pursue them. The defense mechanism is denial. You are living in the illusion that nothing has changed. The pain you are avoiding is the feelings of rejection. The reality is that your friend does not want to be with you, and their actions reveal that fact. It is important to go through the grieving process associated with the loss of this relationship. Even though it is painful, your choice to not use a defense of denial allows you to not believe the lies that you are unworthy.

Playing the victim: Placing blame on something or someone else outside of ourselves instead of taking responsibility for our own problems and emotions.

Pride: "I don't let my emotions bother me" or "I am strong, and I don't need help."

Projectizing: I coined this term for a form of self-hatred that makes oneself a project to fix. It is discussed in detail in chapter 8, "When You Become a Cuckoo."

Fantasizing: Escaping a painful reality by longing for and imagining a different set of circumstances or relationships. It is discussed in greater detail later in this chapter.

Which of these defense mechanisms do you most frequently use? In what ways do they show up in your life currently? What is the painful situation or relationship you are avoiding? What are the emotions you are not feeling?

These questions will assist you in gaining awareness of what defense mechanisms you are using and what pain you are blocking so you can begin to learn to be honest with yourself and honest with others in order to face the true source of your pain and begin to heal and live a more fulfilling and meaningful life instead of a life of suffering.

The Fantasy Cuckoo

The defense mechanism of fantasy has a tendency to fall completely off the radar and is unknown to most, yet it is one of the most powerful and destructive ways to avoid reality. Like the cuckoo, the fantasy defense is an invisible enemy that invades your thought life and taints your God-given imagination in order to sabotage your heart's true desires and twist the truth.

Fantasy leads to suffering when we try to avoid pain and reality by using the defense of denial.

Fantasy begins with a desire, and because we do not have the thing or person we desire in reality, we begin to imagine or fantasize that we do. Essentially, we live in denial. We deny that circumstances and people in our lives cannot always meet our expectations or give us what we want. For example, we can have a pure desire for marriage or to be promoted at work. But when our desires go unmet or something or someone does not turn in our favor as we hoped, we escape the pain of disappointment and rejection by pretending it did not happen and living our life according to the false hope.

Fantasy is using our imagination and thought life to escape the reality of a situation and our corresponding pain rather than facing it. Fantasy is also a falsification of the truth. The truth is conformity to reality, and fantasy is conformity to denial.

God designed our imagination as a powerful, creative function of the right brain as a template to hear from him and to see what he sees. Imagination is also a foundation for vision and faith. But rather than use our imagination for good, we twist it into a defense mechanism so we can live in denial driven by a fear of not getting what we want.

The defense of fantasy is at the root of most addictions. People self-medicate through drugs, alcohol, affairs, and pornography, yet addiction begins in their imagination. They fantasize about their next drink, next escapade, or next movie long before they begin any of these activities. We all have an addiction to denial, to not being present in the here and now.

We often avoid the truth of our life by waiting for our fantasies to become reality, and therefore we lie to ourselves. Rather than end our suffering by running toward the truth, we run toward our cuckoo-coping companions (work, sex, drugs, food). People who have addictions are addicted to denial; they want to escape the current reality because it is painful and scary. They do not want to be in the present moment, so they fantasize about an imaginary future. Their drugs of choice are denial and their fantasies.

Fantasy does not always manifest in addictions, however. Addictions are the most severe form, but fantasy is often more subtle. The fantasy cuckoo is an imposter, a counterfeit, a temporary fix, and it deceives us away from what is true. We create a fantasy in our minds that keeps us feeling safe, needed, loved, special, and important. And like a cuckoo, our fantasies take and take until we are thoroughly disillusioned. Essentially, we are using this defense mechanism of fantasy to deny or escape the reality of pain, loss, disappointment, rejection, or heartbreak.

Usually, given the strength of our denial and our unwillingness to deal properly with reality and our corresponding pain, we have many other buried emotions that drive our fantasy at even deeper and more dangerous levels. This fantasy defense mechanism generally comes from an inner drive to satisfy an unmet need that has existed in our life, perhaps even from childhood. Denial through fantasy has the potential to escalate into destructive urges to achieve fulfillment and satisfaction no matter the cost.

This defense mechanism can begin in childhood because we experienced a trauma and coped with the pain by creating a way out through fantasizing about a different set of circumstances. When the unmet need and unresolved pain carries through to adulthood, and when it is repeated enough, we can become addicted to our fantasies, which keeps us stuck in unhealthy relationships and repeating old, familiar patterns.

Rachel and Her Fantasy Cuckoo

Rachel was cake tasting for her wedding with her mother, sister, and maid of honor when she received the phone call. Her fiancé, Luke, said he needed to talk, and it was important. Her heart sank. A part of her knew the inevitable was approaching, although the stronger part of her was living in denial. She was hoping their engagement would make everything OK.

Luke told her he loved her deeply and considered her his best friend, but he wasn't quite sure if he was still in love with her. In fact, he had developed romantic feelings for someone else, a colleague at work. He said he had really hoped the engagement would solidify his love for Rachel and change his heart toward his colleague, but he nonetheless was beginning to feel trapped and increasingly anxious. He told Rachel he needed to explore his feelings for this other woman, whom he had considered a friend for so many years. Rachel had met this colleague while attending various work events, happy hours, and holiday parties over the years and had also overheard their phone conversations. She intuitively had a bad feeling about their work relationship and confronted Luke several times, yet she also desperately wanted to believe they were simply work friends.

Luke called off the wedding. He said he needed time and space to do some soul-searching. Rachel was ashamed, devastated, and heartbroken. Because the pain was intense, she began coping with her loss of both her fiancé and her dream of marriage by developing a fantasy to numb her pain. She fantasized how he would come back for her and realize the error of his ways, how he had made a horrible mistake. He would proclaim his love for Rachel, realizing that the other woman was nothing compared to Rachel and that his feelings for the other woman weren't love but lust. As a result of her fantasy, she put her life on hold and waited for Luke.

Besides, she rationalized, he was honest with her about needing some time, so maybe he was right, he just needed some space to come to his senses. Or once his soul-searching season was over, he would be ready to make a commitment to marriage. She fantasized many different conversations they would have and imagined many scenarios of him surprising her and coming back for her. She even fantasized about how this entire situation could bring them even closer together than before, and they would tell this story to their children one day.

Rachel began to believe the lies she was telling herself, and her denial grew stronger and stronger. In the meantime, Luke avoided her phone calls. She even spiritualized away her pain by believing this must be God's plan for their love story, and she just had to be patient and wait for him. Rachel was stuck. She was trapped in her fantasies caused by her denial.

Her underlying pain of sadness, rejection, heartbreak, and abandonment fueled her denial of reality that Luke had left her and that he said he might be in love with another woman. She never stopped to consider why she would want to marry a man like that! Instead, she hung on to the one wisp of hope she strongly believed she was hearing from him: "I need time to figure all this out."

She did not need to let go of Luke; he had already left. She needed to let go of her fantasy. She needed to accept the reality that she was single and not getting married to Luke. Her fantasy defense mechanism was blocking her pain. She was living in denial. Rachel was suffering.

Her cuckoo was not Luke or Luke's leaving; it was her fantasy of him coming back.

The truth is that she had been suffering in her relationship with Luke for years prior to their engagement. She could never quite trust him, especially regarding his relationship with his work colleague. Something seemed off. He spent longer hours at work. He slowly stopped pursuing Rachel, and she no longer felt special to him or a priority in his life.

By denying reality, she was unable to deal with her pain of abandonment in a healthy manner and grieve the loss of her fiancé. It was easier for her to relate to her fantasy instead, as she had very painful feelings of rejection over this loss. She was suffering because she had put her life and dreams on hold and waited for him.

Through our counseling sessions, Rachel was able to face reality, let go of her fantasy, heal from her rejection and abandonment wounds, and embrace the grieving process. All of this gave her the freedom to enjoy her life again and trust God with her heart's desires.

Years after her treatment ended, Rachel reached out to thank me for helping her see the truth during her sessions as well as to share a photo from her wedding day. She explained in her note that once she let go of the fantasy cuckoo of Luke coming back, she found herself and truly enjoyed the company. She ended up marrying a wonderful man who was in her life all along, yet she had never noticed him while she was living in denial and caught up in her fantasies about Luke.

The Fantasy Friend

When working with my clients who avoid reality through the defense mechanism of fantasizing, we call the object of their fantasy their fantasy friend.

The fantasy friend does not have to be an addictive behavior. The fantasy friend can be any type of cuckoo and distraction in your life that you tend to turn to and fantasize about when you are having a bad day or struggling.

For example, a woman is feeling inadequate among her skinny friends or perhaps she was recently rejected by a love interest and begins fantasizing about what she would look like five or ten pounds lighter, what she would wear, whom she would impress, and how powerful she would feel. At this point, there is no addiction, she does not have an eating disorder, and she is not addicted to weight-loss supplements or drugs, at least for now. However, the fantasy is still a subtle inter-ruption of her life and begins to interfere with her thoughts and emotions. She feels inadequate and ashamed because she is believing the lie that her worth is tied to her appearance. This fantasy cuckoo consumes her as she continually feeds it by entertaining these images rather than honestly facing her feelings of inadequacy or rejection.

After a few sessions with my clients, I take them through the following exercise. I invite you to join me here as well.

Your fantasy friend comforts you. When you feel hurt, rejected, abandoned, ashamed, anxious, jealous, or inadequate, your fantasy friend will want to make you feel better. The fantasy friend is seductive, as all cuckoos are. The fantasy friend calls out to you, woos you, and draws you into denying your current reality, that is, the painful situation or relationship you are currently in. You fantasize by indulging, creating, and entertaining thoughts, ideas, conversations, or imaginations that are not real, but they fuel your denial.

First identify the painful situation you are trying to deny or pretend doesn't exist:

_____

_____

_____

What or who is your fantasy friend that you turn to?

_____

_____

_____

What painful emotions is your fantasy friend helping you to avoid?

_____

_____

_____

Your fantasy friend has been around for a while, knows you well, and feels familiar. But when you are hurt, you must make the decision to not engage with your fantasy friend. Your fantasy friend is depriving you of your God-given imagination. The fantasy friend blocks you from hearing God's voice, receiving truth, and experiencing real comfort.

Your fantasy friend is a quick, temporary fix. Your fantasy friend leaves you vulnerable to the Enemy, to lies, and to cuckoos, because you are abiding in an illusion and clinging to your fantasy instead of clinging to the truth.

Make a choice to no longer turn to your fantasy friend for comfort. Take a stand for truth and face your hurt by inviting God into your pain and asking him to speak to you his words and to reveal his vision for your life. Eventually, your fantasy friend will no longer hold you captive and keep you stuck in a continual cycle of suffering. Begin to say no to your fantasy friend and yes to God, yes to truth, and yes to freedom.

Cuckoo-Coping Companions

When we block our pain through defense mechanisms over a prolonged period, the real pain is still there, beneath the surface. The pain is buried alive and will manifest somewhere eventually. Meanwhile, we turn to cuckoo-coping companions such as food, sex, work, television, affairs, gambling, gossip, social media, planning, shopping, alcohol and drugs, and sleep.

Cuckoo-coping companions are pain-numbing agents, ways we numb our pain and distract ourselves. They mimic companions because they comfort us temporarily when things become hard and painful. However, these companions are not good friends; they are imposters and self-inflicted cuckoos.

Maybe you have recently lost your job, gone through a divorce or a bad breakup, or regret a missed opportunity to pursue a dream. To avoid feeing sad, lonely, and afraid, you make daily choices to numb your pain by overeating, overworking, overdrinking, and overperforming. We become addicted to our cuckoo-coping companions because they distract us and prevent us from truly feeling our uncomfortable and painful emotions. But if we turn to these coping companions regularly for comfort, they start to significantly impair other areas of our lives physically, spiritualty, and socially.

For example, your husband has new work assignments, and he is traveling more frequently, including weekends. You begin drinking more in the evenings to cope with your stress of having to operate more like a single parent in addition to your increased household responsibilities. When your husband asks how you are feeling about the transition, you tell him how thankful you are he has this job that provides for your family and that you will make it work. Although this is true, you are avoiding communicating honestly how you are really feeling. Perhaps you fear there is nothing you can do to change the circumstances. Drinking to cope and ignore your underlying pain or pretending like nothing is wrong eventually creates more suffering than the pain itself, such as addictive behaviors and marital issues.

Which cuckoo-coping companions are you turning to in order to hide from your pain?

The Cuckoo Syndrome Cycle Exposed

We cannot change our painful circumstances, but we can learn to identify lies, defense mechanisms, and cuckoo-coping companions. Becoming aware of our patterns does not mean they will automatically disappear, but they will no longer be able to hide from you or deceive you. Now that these cuckoos, these invisible enemies, are visible, you will be able to see them as self-inflicted cycles and refuse to nurture them in your life. As you dismantle their strongholds brick by brick, thought by thought, defense by defense, fantasy friend by fantasy friend, they will eventually lose their power over you. When you reject the lies and false beliefs,

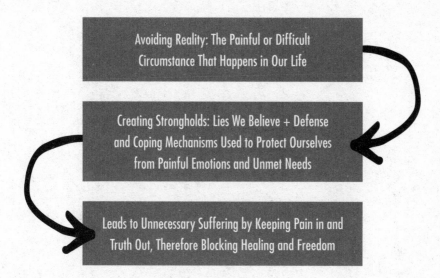

you make room in your nest, your life, to receive and know the truth that will set you free from the cuckoo's snare.

CHAPTER 6

THE FEAR CUCKOO

A Subtle Cuckoo in Disguise

The only thing we have to fear is . . . fear itself.
—FRANKLIN D. ROOSEVELT

FEAR IS A PART OF THE HUMAN EXPERIENCE AND A NORMAL part of life. But fear can adopt the nature of a cuckoo when it comes in as an imposter, an invisible enemy. This is because the way fears show up and create unnecessary suffering is not always apparent. Fear is an undercurrent of the Cuckoo Syndrome and can subtly disguise itself in the following forms: the control cuckoo, the anxiety cuckoo, the busyness cuckoo, the stress cuckoo, and the most cunning cuckoo of all, the serpent cuckoo.

Fear can manifest physically, emotionally, or spiritually ("a spirit of fear," 2 Tim. 1:7). Fear is a powerful emotion stored in the brain's amygdala, alerting us to the threat of harm to help us survive by protecting us from danger. In this case, fear can help us to avoid or leave hurtful or abusive relationships with cuckoos. Alternatively, our hidden, unchecked fears can do the opposite, causing us to believe we are not good enough, which attracts cuckoos.

This chapter specifically focuses on the ways fear can harm us. Fear can be crippling and tormenting and has the potential to steal our true self and suffocate our purpose, much like a cuckoo. Living in a constant state of anxiety and stress can erode our careers, our ministries, and our most intimate relationships, including the relationship we have with ourselves.

The Control Cuckoo: An Obsessive Need to Know

I explain to my clients that the need to control is rooted in fear. Fear can look like being overly controlling, which manifests in relationships with others, at work, or in our daily life routines and thinking patterns. Often we want control during moments of uncertainty and pain and when we are feeling unsafe and insecure. One way control can manifest itself is in an obsessive need to know, which creates mental torment and toxic overthinking through ruminating, rationalizing, and reasoning.

The Tree of Knowledge

The need to know is an age-old problem. In the book of Genesis, we read that God instructed Adam and Eve not to eat from the Tree of the Knowledge of Good and Evil. So what is it about the Tree of the Knowledge of Good and Evil that they were asked by God not to partake of? And why was the serpent so interested in tempting Eve to eat from it?

Eve's conversation with the serpent caused her to begin to contemplate "you will be like God, knowing good and evil" (Gen. 3:5). The temptation for God-like knowledge was still present even though all her needs were met and she was created in his image and likeness. Eve began to doubt God's goodness and believed the lie that God was withholding something from her (knowledge). Eve then saw that the tree was desirable to make her wise. As soon as she and Adam ate of the tree, they had knowledge, but only of their nakedness: "And they knew that they were naked" and felt ashamed (Gen. 3:7). Their human understanding of "wise" was limited and was not dependent on their Creator.

Our knowledge in and of itself, apart from God, does not produce life (the Tree of Life). Adam and Eve replaced life and a relationship with their Creator with knowledge and made knowledge their god from that day forward, which led to the fall. The Tree of the Knowledge of Good and Evil separated them from God, and they became self-conscious and hid themselves.

The Enemy's tactics to tempt us and engage us in conversations that are based in a lie are still present today, just as our desire for knowledge apart from our Creator is still a temptation. When we try to become like God in our knowledge, we open ourselves up for God's Word to be twisted, and we believe lies instead of the truth.

God Is Bigger than Your Understanding

Trust in the LORD *with all your heart, and lean*
not on your own understanding; in all your ways
acknowledge Him, and He shall direct your paths.
Do not be wise in your own eyes. (PROV. 3:5–7)

There is a connection between trusting God and not leaning on our own understanding, not being wise in our own eyes apart from acknowledging him in all our ways and letting him direct us. Faith does not require understanding. Many times we trust God only when we understand what he is doing, but whatever God is doing, it does not need to make sense to us for it to make sense to God. We do not need to understand why God does or does not do certain things. Can you choose to obey him anyway?

We say, "I don't understand why this is happening, God." Whatever is happening does not need our understanding. It exists whether we understand it or not. If we understood everything perfectly, we would not need to rely on God; we would rely on ourselves and our knowledge. In both my personal life and clinical experience with clients, I've discovered a powerful truth: we do not know ourselves by ourselves. This means we do not fully know ourselves alone unless we have an objective person to help us to see things we cannot see within ourselves, our blind spots.

The good news is we serve a God who is full of grace, compassion, and wisdom and who intimately knows us and is pursuing us often. He asks, "Where are you?" (Gen. 3:9). God knows where we are, yet he invites us back into relating with him and trusting him so we can know the truth, which will set us free.

There is more on how to identify and defeat the serpent's cunning strategies in the final section of this chapter, "The Serpent Cuckoo."

Why We Ask "Why?"

The question I hear most from my clients when they are afraid and trying to control certain areas of their lives is "Why?" "Why doesn't my spouse understand me?" "Why will nobody help me begin my ministry?" "Why hasn't God healed me?" "Why can't I find my dream job?" These why questions are motivated from a place of fear and such underlying emotions as anger and sadness that they are afraid to address. The why questions are more about needing to know an answer than about understanding their pain or how to get unstuck. Their obsessive need to get an answer separates them from their true selves because they are so busy trying to figure out the intellectual answers to their questions, they can avoid dealing with their deeper, innermost heart issues and desires.

Spiritually speaking, have you ever noticed that the one question God doesn't answer is "Why?" I have noticed this in my life and in the lives of my clients, especially when why is asked out of a place of pain and fear. Why often provides a diversion from our emotions, because we don't want to feel, we want to know. This is dangerous as it disconnects us from ourselves, others, and even God.

In the following passage from *A Grief Observed*, C. S. Lewis shared his revelations about God's silence with regard to his unanswered questions:

> *When I lay these questions before God I get no answer. But a rather special sort of "No answer." It is not the locked door. It is more like a silent, certainly not uncompassionate, gaze. As though He shook His head not in refusal but waiving the question. Like, "Peace, child; you don't understand."*
>
> *Can a mortal ask questions which God finds unanswerable? Quite easily, I should think. All nonsense questions are unanswerable. How many hours are in a mile? Is yellow square*

or round? Probably half the questions we ask—half our great
theological and metaphysical questions—are like that.[19]

What a powerful description of how our questions come
across to God. There is no answer to "Is yellow square or round?"
because yellow is not a shape, it's a color. So perhaps our question
to God, "Why does my spouse not understand me?" comes across
that way. We don't know what we don't know. In time, with trust
and maturity, we will grow in our faith and understanding.

As C. S. Lewis stated, when we ask God questions, it comes
across to him as unanswerable because our questions are coming
from a childlike place. We do not yet have all the necessary
wisdom and experience to see things from his perspective. Peace
is obtained from knowing that God is not refusing to answer our
questions, and Scripture assures us that he gives us a peace that
transcends our understanding (Phil. 4:7). Peace requires childlike
faith in our heavenly Father during the times when we don't know
and when we do know.

Rest assured there will never be a time God doesn't care for
and listen to you. "Why?" is never a question you need to ask
because there is always something for God to reveal to you in
terms of your purpose, even amid the challenges you face and the
pains you endure.

Personally, I've found I am too busy asking God questions
about things, and he is more interested in having a relationship
with me. If I use my knowledge to understand God's wisdom, I
can go no further than what I understand. It is important to learn
the powerful truth that our Father knows our needs even before
we ask him (Matt. 6:8).

When I sit with clients who are desperately wanting to
know why and trying to control some area of their life, I help

them identify what they are afraid of in that situation and where they feel out of control so they can overcome the fear and let go of the ways they seek to control. Eventually, as they learn, heal, and grow in their faith, they realize how they feel hurt and that obsessively pursuing answers isn't as comforting as they thought. Because what they thought they needed to know created more doubt and more suffering than not having the answers.

We might still be tempted to control and be afraid, but we can believe God is with us. We may be relinquishing control, but we can trust in our Creator who is in control. We may not know the future, but God's plans are to prosper us and not harm us, to give us a hope and a future (Jer. 29:11).

An obsessive need to know that is rooted in fear traps us into using knowledge we do not yet have to predict the future that is not ours to know. The need to know can also be rooted in the fear of tomorrow.

The Anxiety Cuckoo: A Fear of Tomorrow

Do not worry about tomorrow, for tomorrow will worry about its own things. Sufficient for the day is its own trouble. (MATT. 6:34)

Anxiety is closely related to fear, but in a more sophisticated, rational way, it is rooted in an ability to anticipate future harm or threat, whereas fear is a physiological reaction in response to harm, a fight-or-flight response. Often the cause of anxiety is a preoccupation with the thought of danger being perceived as not real. Anxious people tend to anticipate harm often where there is little or none.

The most prevalent types of fear my clients have that create anxiety are fears of rejection and abandonment, failure, intimacy and commitment, change, uncertainty and the unknown, being alone, missing out, illness and death, and pain. The "fear of" meaning it has not yet happened.

The physical symptoms of anxiety are very real even though the threat is perceived. When people are suffering with anxiety, they can show such physiological symptoms as frequent body pain (nausea, upset stomach, headaches, muscle tension), sweating, dizziness, trembling, or rapid heartbeat.

The common warning signs of anxiety include isolating and avoiding certain situations, excessive worrying about what others think, and normal responsibilities feeling overwhelming. Additional signs include sleep issues and nightmares, restlessness, agitation, obsessive planning, overly controlling, a constant sense of dread, difficulty concentrating and making decisions, chronic fatigue, and avoiding social situations. Most of my clients do not realize their anxiety is a normal part of their everyday life as this way of being becomes who they are. These are all cuckoos that consume all their time and attention and overtake their personality and thwart the joyful, purposeful life God destined them to live for.

Anxiety is a normal part of what it means to be human. Anxiety is a signal. As you learn to name your condition as anxiety, you can begin the healing process so that your anxiety is not debilitating. In this way anxiety can be a helpful indicator that tells us there are important underlying issues and buried emotions, lies we have accepted that need our attention so we can replace them with truth and have peace of mind. It is important to slow down and pay attention so our anxiety is not debilitating and affecting our everyday life.

Don't Suffer Twice: Borrowing Trouble Mentally

I tell my clients who are dealing with anxiety, "Don't suffer twice." By that, I mean that we don't want to borrow trouble mentally by tormenting ourselves through toxic overthinking. This occurs through imagining worst-case scenarios, rehearsing conversations, obsessing over details, ruminating, scheming, perfecting, and overanalyzing.

The Bible says to "take therefore *no thought* for the morrow" (Matt. 6:34 KJV, emphasis added). Anxiety begins as a thought, and then our body reacts. We suffer immensely in our thought life and imaginations, and the thing we are afraid of has not even happened in reality. Remember, we suffer when we avoid truth, avoid reality.

The emotion of fear arises with a threat of harm, either physical or emotional, real or imagined. Anxiety typically begins as a thought that produces apprehensiveness and uneasiness of mind, and then our body responds: increased heart rate, sweating, muscle tension. Anxiety specifically is about perceiving the future. For this reason, anxiety takes us out of the present; it is not possible to be anxious and in the present moment.

People lose sight of the truth that they are resilient, wise, and capable. They become plagued with self-doubt about their capacity to cope with a potentially harmful or painful situation. They fail to remember God will be their ever-present help in times of need. If what we fear does happen, we will have the tools, support, and knowledge we need in the time we need it. And if it is painful, hard, and scary, then we will deal with it then, not now—if it really occurs.

Anxiety is about trying to predict the future and all the terrible things that could happen before they actually happen, with the false hope that we will not suffer as much. The truth is that we are suffering now.

What If?

I've noticed when my clients are suffering with anxiety, they tend to ruminate on what-if questions. What-ifs are rooted in negative expectations (expecting something bad to happen). Therefore, every what-if question is an inaccurate attempt at predicting the future:

- What if I cannot pay my bills?
- What if I never have children?
- What if I never get married?
- What if my spouse leaves me?
- What if I never belong?
- What if I never get healed?

It is tough to recognize what-if questions as anxiety. These questions are quite convincing because we come across a present moment situation that is scary.

For example, Andrew moved into a new home in his dream neighborhood with his wife and children. He had his eye on this neighborhood for years, waiting for the right house for sale at the right price at the right time. After settling in and enjoying his new home and making precious memories, he was going on an evening run around the neighborhood and noticed some construction a few streets over from his house. A row of older homes was being torn down and newer homes were being built. Andrew was not surprised because his neighborhood was highly sought after due to its woodsy, private, and quaint characteristics.

Suddenly, Andrew become overwhelmed with anxiety: his heart raced, he had sweaty palms, he felt dizzy, and he was short of breath. He began imagining the older homes on either side of his house being torn down and these new monstrosities towering above his home, removing all the big, beautiful trees surrounding him, just as he was currently witnessing.

His thoughts began to race. *What if they begin construction on my street? What if moving here was a mistake? What if I didn't hear God correctly? What if the construction noise is so loud and goes on for months and months? What if I never enjoy another moment of peace, quiet, and privacy on my screen porch? What if my new neighbors take down the large, beautiful trees? What if the loud construction noise affects my job since I work from home full time?* And on and on.

The construction Andrew was experiencing down the street was happening. It was loud and disruptive, and the street looked completely different. He had empathy and compassion for the neighbors next to whom these monstrosities were going up, towering above them, blocking their view, and the big, beautiful trees beingcut down, eliminating privacy.

As often as the opportunity presented itself, Andrew made a point on his evening runs to ask his neighbors if they had heard any news of this happening on their street. His evening runs, once his place of relief, peace, and perspective, became consumed by this issue. He was losing sleep and it distracted him during the day. Andrew became highly anxious.

The reality is that no houses on his street were being torn down. His anxiety sabotaged the joy of his new home and became a cuckoo that invaded his life. It blocked him from being present with his family and work. The anxiety he was experiencing was costly because what he feared had not truly occurred.

By working through his anxiety, Andrew realized that anticipating the future was frustrating him and his family, and he was suffering unnecessarily. He was able to face his fears and believe that if what he imagined occurred in the present, he would be OK and know what to do because he was resilient, strong, and capable of making wise decisions.

Anxiety is about the future—anticipating negative events and worst-case scenarios. Anxiety is anticipating the future without God in it.

When you are experiencing anxiety, ask yourself, *What are these feelings trying to tell me? What are my what-if questions? How am I suffering now, even though what I am afraid of has not actually happened yet? What worst-case scenarios am I imagining? What would this situation look like if God were in it?*

The Busyness Cuckoo

For years my typical response was, "I'd love to, but I'm crazy busy right now." My greatest desire was to be alone and numb out in front of the television. I realized this was no way to live. I had filled my schedule to the point where I was not enjoying life. I was busy, but I was not joyful.

Busyness is a habitual and compulsive state of doing rather than a state of being. I find too many people move through life always *busy*, going from one thing to the next. Many pride themselves on having social calendars scheduled several months in advance. Others congratulate themselves on how few hours of sleep they need each night, how successful they are at work, how they have tried every new restaurant and winery and been to every concert, traveled to every major city, or how important they are socially among their friends.

Chronic busyness leads to anxiety, stress, workaholism, burnout, isolation, and perfectionism. Perfectionism is rooted in fear and takes our passions and turns them into obsessions that become all-consuming. (There is more to come on perfectionism in chapter 7, "The Perfectionism Cuckoo: When Passions Become Obsessions.")

Eventually, the prolonged stress of busyness will impact your health and limit your God-given purpose, and your relationships will suffer.

Busy people keep their phone attached to them as if it were an extension of their body, checking social media every free second, drowning out their own inner voice vying for attention. This pattern can become a self-inflicted cuckoo when it consumes all of your thought life, time, attention, and emotional energy. All the while, you leave no room for your soul to breathe, your mind to wander, your heart to feel, your senses to enjoy the beauty of nature, or your spirit to know God's voice. You allow social media, to-do lists, and busyness to choose everything for you.

Having no plans, taking the time to rest, and being still are not necessarily signs of idleness, wasted time, or laziness, as busy people frequently perceive. They are keys to living a truly fulfilled life. So many people live for the weekend and dread Mondays, are dissatisfied with their jobs even though they are successful, and lack true passion, meaning, and purpose.

Mastering the practice of rest has taken me years. Now, life for me is about being and not doing. It's about enjoying the little things. Solitude and simplicity are words I have come to embrace wholeheartedly. I have taken the time to see beauty in simplicity, marvel at the precious gifts of everyday life, and celebrate these quiet, unexpected moments in all their wonder. I get wildly enthusiastic about little things. It has taken me a while to overcome the disease of busyness, and this new life-style requires living in the present moment, not going from one task to the next.

We must resist the cuckoo of busyness, as busyness is often a manifestation of anxiety, the fear of missing out, the fear of rejection, and the fear of failure. Many people feel the need to be busy, falsely believing they are in control of their lives and accepting the lie that busyness will take away their pain. They become obsessive about filling their schedules, which eventually become an idol in their life, an idol of accomplishments.

Busy people are compulsive planners who have a never-ending to-do list of things that must get done so they feel needed, wanted, and respected. They feel as though once they check everything off their to-do list, then they can rest and be at peace. Their mind becomes distracted, and they are constantly preoccupied with planning the next best thing.

The temptation for these people, myself included, is very strong and very real. It requires embracing the art of rest, addressing underlying fears and insecurities, and resisting the temptation to say yes all the time. The reality is that a person cannot hear properly when they are chronically busy. They cannot hear their own heart and intuition, hear the wise counsel of others, and hear God. When our minds are too busy, we become distracted and miss the still, calm, quiet moments God is using to reveal helpful truth to us through his Spirit.

Rest does not always equate to sleep. Rest can be a physical time-out, but rest is also Spirit-directed activity: "A man's heart plans his way, but the LORD directs his steps" (Prov. 16:9). This means you can invite the Holy Spirit to show you what things you can let go of that you are doing out of fear or because of a need to please, perform, and perfect.

There will always be seasons of life where we are busier than other times, and this is normal. The busyness cuckoo refers to a chronic state of perpetual busyness that neglects other areas of life, causes harm to yourself, and affects your relationships with others. It takes over a person's life and produces dangerous levels of stress.

In fact, even in the seasons when you are required to be busier than usual for necessary reasons, it is possible to be busy and still at rest. Rest in this case means mentally, emotionally, and spiritually at rest; for example, freedom from compulsive planning, freedom from having to figure out everything on your own, and freedom from trying to control circumstances that are beyond your control. Rest is about balance, peace of mind, and a deep-seated joy of the soul. Jesus will never give you more than you can handle, and he will show you how to rest.

Start asking yourself what you can eliminate from your life. It may even be some good things that are just not the best things for you right now. If you feel you are being driven by busyness, stop the dangerous flow of adrenaline by taking a time-out. Go for a walk outside. Enjoy a cup of tea. Take a nap. Find a pleasurable activity. Watch a movie. Bake. Call a friend. Read a book. Take a step of faith and do something else that is restful and brings you true joy.

Jesus told his disciples, "Come aside by yourselves to a deserted place and rest a while" (Mark 6:31). The Greek word for "rest" in this verse is *anapauo*, which means "to make to cease." It describes a cessation from toil, a refreshment, an intermission.[20] Is it time for you to take an intermission?

The Stress Cuckoo: Not Listening to Your Body

Some of my clients came to counseling because their medical doctors advised them to begin psychotherapy to address mental health issues and their emotional life. Typically, they have depression, anxiety, or stress. Some clients have seen a plethora of doctors who are unable to identify a measurable cause for their illness and have no diagnosis for them, leaving them without answers for their unexplained medical symptoms. They can be struggling with chronic migraines, back pain, or stomach issues, for example. Medical doctors frequently attribute illness and disease to stress. An alarmingly high percentage of diseases is stress-related.

Unresolved emotions can show up in our bodies, so ignoring our body's pain signals is a way we can deceive ourselves. We can lie to ourselves in our thought life by making excuses, justifying our busy lifestyle, convincing ourselves everything is fine, denying there's any stress in our life, yet our body will tell the truth.

The stress cuckoo is an invisible enemy most people live with daily and suffer silently under its toxic weight. Therefore, it is so important to pay attention to our bodies and the wisdom God intended for them to provide.

Cuckoos Lie, but Your Body Tells the Truth

Ignoring our bodies becomes a self-inflicted cuckoo because we are engaging in sabotaging behaviors and toxic thinking patterns, deceiving ourselves that we are OK when in fact our bodies tell us just the opposite. Ignoring our stress keeps us stuck in a perpetual cycle of suffering.

Alternatively, being in a cuckoo relationship with another person who is insatiable and consistently manipulating you to take care of their every need is all consuming. Continually neglecting yourself to please them leads a person into dangerous places of stress due to mental, emotional, and physical exhaustion.

Our true selves get lost when we are in a cuckoo relationship. Our bodies disclose to us the facts, correct information, about who we really are, what we want, and what we need, and we must not avoid this information rationally with our minds. Essentially, the physical symptoms we experience always tell us the truth even when we lie to ourselves: "I am not that anxious, busy, stressed, or controlling." Yet our body aches and pains bring to light the reality, no matter what reasons we come up with or what excuses we make.

No matter how hard we try to ignore our bodies, we cannot get rid of the evidence our bodies contain. By choosing to continually ignore our body's warning signals—such symptoms of anxiety as headaches, muscle aches, and fatigue—we leave ourselves susceptible to suffering from more serious health conditions, illnesses, and chronic pain.

To cope with stress, we can turn to cuckoo-coping companions to medicate our stress by numbing and temporarily easing our pain with a cocktail of pills, alcohol, smoking, and overeating. These ways of coping are subtle at first. Perhaps we consume large amounts of caffeine to make it through the day without collapsing, we have one too many glasses of wine to wind down at night, we dread going to bed at night due to persistent sleep issues, and we dread waking up due to being overworked, overscheduled, and overwhelmed.

Developing anxiety symptoms is common for people who are stressed. Anxiety symptoms are real and can lead to various mental health disorders when left untreated. When you are stressed, you are constantly on high alert, as your body is pumping out high levels of cortisol. Eventually your body will tell you something is wrong. Burying painful emotions and associated fears is powerful and often happens unconsciously. At times, we experience physical symptoms because our mind considers them to be less painful, less scary, and less harmful than our painful emotions. Therefore, listening to our bodies is so important.

Overcoming stress requires us to face our fears and deal with the underlying root of why our lives are filled with toxic stress. As we begin to heal, we make the decision to resist the temptation to push ourselves to the point of exhaustion, and we learn to set boundaries and take care of ourselves. If you find yourself reverting to old patterns of stress, find hope in the fact that it is a normal part of the healing process, and your body will always point you back to the truth.

You can begin to live from a place of rest and peace rather than fear and stress as you begin to listen to the wisdom of your body.

The Serpent Cuckoo

"Now the serpent was more cunning than any beast of the field which the LORD God had made" (Gen. 3:1). Satan tempted Adam and Eve in the same way he tempts us today. How does he tempt us? He deceitfully twists God's Word.

Satan is the grand cuckoo. He is a liar and master manipulator. Like the cuckoo, he seeks to deceive you with a lie about the level of danger he wants you to think you have been exposed to. When we begin to question the Word of God and doubt his goodness, this creates fear.

Do not give Satan more power than is necessary; after all, it was Eve who ate the apple. Satan did not force her to do so. The point here is to recognize the spiritual component of fear, and "we don't want to unwittingly give Satan an opening for yet more mischief—we're not oblivious to his sly ways" (2 Cor. 2:11 MSG).

Did God Say?

Satan plays a major role in creating fear, and his schemes have not changed from what's depicted in the garden of Eden in Genesis 3. His schemes are crafty and subtle, insinuating God is not trustworthy. He twists the word of God either from Scripture or what he is speaking to us personally through the Holy Spirit.

Satan poses the question "Did God say?" to cause us to doubt the goodness of God and deceive us into believing he is withholding something good. As a result, we draw conclusions based on lies and make destructive choices by relying on our own knowledge. We rush ahead of God's timing, sacrifice our values, and pursue things God never intended us to pursue.

Did God say he will provide for you and take care of your needs? You are not going to be able to pay your bills again this month. You might as well get used to living paycheck to paycheck. Your house will go into foreclosure.

Did God say your marriage will be repaired and that you will enjoy one another? Your spouse is not in love with you anymore. Now that you have children, you will lose the romance. You will keep living as roommates. It is too late.

Did God say he will give you the desires of your heart for a new job/career/ministry? You will never really enjoy your work. Other people are more qualified; you have been out of work too long. You cannot be a parent and have a successful, fulfilling career or ministry. Your dream job is not going to happen. You will always dread Mondays and live for the weekends.

Did God say he forgives you? You've really messed up this time. His grace will not cover this mistake. God's unconditional love does not apply to you in this area anymore. God will not forgive you again.

Did God say you will have close friends in your community? The reason your friends are not initiating getting together with you anymore is not because they are busy; it's because you are too much. They are getting tired of you.

Did God say you will get married? You're too old. You're too picky. Your children won't accept a stepparent. You're not attractive enough. You will always be lonely. You will be single forever. Your past is too complicated. You work too much. You're not putting yourself out there enough.

Did God say your children will be OK? They will fall into a bad crowd and will lose their values. They will start drinking and doing drugs. They don't like you anymore. They are going to be bullied at school. They will keep secrets from you.

Did God say he will heal you? You've been praying, yet you are still not healed. Your faith is not strong enough. God must be punishing you. His heart is not truly for you. He heals other people, but not you.

Satan hovers over your circumstances and mocks what God has said to you. We must speak the truth during Satan's schemes and stand on the promises of God when the Father of Lies comes to mock and deceive us. Amid doubt and fear, we must face the Enemy head-on by declaring God's Word whether our circumstances line up with the truth *yet.*

Because he is "a liar and the father of it" and "there is *no* truth in him" (John 8:44, emphasis added), we can discount every "Did God say" question he poses.

Continue to stand in faith until the manifestation comes: "Having done all, to stand" (Eph. 6:13). Continue to stand when you do not see God's Word work immediately. Be patient. Find confidence that God is working behind the scenes on your behalf: "I don't think the way you think. The way you work isn't the way I work. . . . The words that come out of my mouth [do] not come back empty-handed. They'll do the work I sent them to do, they'll complete the assignment I gave them" (Isa. 55:8, 11 MSG).

Fear Drives and Faith Guides

Rather than getting rid of our fear, we can learn to face our fear, change our mindset about the fears, and address it in healthy ways. Many people falsely believe that to be free of fear or to be delivered from fear means they never experience fear. This is not true; however, we can learn how fear shows up and not allow it to drive us in unhealthy ways.

The control cuckoo, the anxiety cuckoo, the busyness cuckoo, the stress cuckoo, and the serpent cuckoo show up as invisible enemies with their subtle disguises of fear that deceive you and leave you suffering.

It has been said that the phrases "Do not fear," "Do not be afraid," and "Fear not" are referenced in the Bible 365 times.[21] That is one for every day of the year. The fear cuckoo cannot invade your life unless you allow it room to do so. Feeding your fears and allowing your thoughts and imaginations to run wild are self-sabotaging acts.

Are You Thinking About What You Are Thinking About?

Anxiety begins as a thought, which is why it is important to take every thought captive. Thoughts are not facts. Just because a thought enters your mind does not mean it is true. Do not passively accept every thought that comes into your mind. Anxious thoughts can accumulate in your mind and become a stronghold of toxic thinking patterns that keep you locked in a prison of fear.

The opposite of fear is faith. Faith uses our imagination for good, whereas fear through anxiety uses our imagination to predict worst-case scenarios. We are not in control of our future; God is, and he promises us our future is good (Jer. 29:11).

Experiencing fear or anxiety does not mean you lack faith. A destructive thing to say to yourself or another person is to tell them they would stop being anxious or afraid if they had enough faith. We all experience fear; it is normal and human.

What is faith?

"Now faith is the substance of things hoped for, the evidence of things not seen" (Heb. 11:1). This verse appears to describe faith as a deeply rooted conviction about the proof of things that have not yet happened but for which we hope. Essentially, faith has substance. Faith is a confidence and an assurance that we can trust in God and his promises.

Hope is an important element of faith. Hope and faith are not emotions; they are a way of thinking and acting. They are not always warm, fuzzy feelings. Emotions play a role, but faith is grounded in truth and believing the Word of God. Our faith in God provides us the wisdom and strength we need to take the necessary steps to deal with our fears.

Taking steps of faith is doing the opposite of what you fear. Start by imagining best-case scenarios instead of worst-case scenarios. I purposely expect good things—even great things!—to happen in my life. I ask myself, *What would be the exact opposite of this negative expectation or anxious thought?* and I choose to believe that and expect only God's best for me. If something painful happens in the future, I also trust God will be there to help get me through. "Though I walk through the valley of the shadow of death, I will fear no evil; for You are with me; Your rod and Your staff, they comfort me" (Ps. 23:4). We walk through, not around.

Take risks. Pursue the very thing you are afraid of, whether it is proposing to the love of your life, speaking at your church in front of the congregation, being the project lead at work, writing a book, starting a business, beginning a Bible study, going back to school, moving to your dream city, or adopting a child.

Stop placing your dreams and desires on hold because the fear cuckoo has convinced you that this is all your life could become. Don't believe the lie. Do not live under the toxic weight of the fear cuckoo and allow it to smother your heart's true desires.

You will discover your purpose on the other side of your fear.

CHAPTER 7

THE PERFECTIONISM CUCKOO

When Passions Become Obsessions

Anything worth doing is worth doing badly.
—G. K. CHESTERTON

PERFECTIONISM HAS ALWAYS BEEN MY BIGGEST SELF-IN-flicted cuckoo. Here is an example of perfectionism hitting me directly in the face. I was in the final phase of pursuing my profession as a licensed counselor, and I had completed my residency and an arduous application process. After a couple of years, finally, the moment arrived: I could begin preparing for the board exam. The journey to this point was a victory, as it required a bachelor's degree in psychology, a master's degree in clinical counseling, a three-thousand-hour residency (including 250 hours of supervision), and passing the board of counseling licensure exam. As you can imagine, I was relieved the process was ending.

I went into this final step of studying for the board exam both exhilarated and terrified. But I did not spend nearly as much time preparing as I should have, as I was advised to do. I thought I would pass this with no problem. My pride went before my fall.

I clicked "Submit" on my computer screen and I was excited as I pranced over to the proctor to receive my results, which were to be immediately reported as pass or fail. I was utterly devastated and disbelieving when the proctor handed me my results: fail. I nearly fainted. I was a few points from passing. To make matters worse, my significant other, who had driven me to the exam and had given me a card reading, "I look forward to celebrating your victory together," was waiting for me at a coffee shop around the corner. I immediately wished I had come alone, was single again, and could disappear. My pride was shattered.

I had to wait four months before I could retake the exam, and let me tell you, I *really* studied this time around. However, it was not just intense studying that occurred during those four months. I experienced a season of conviction. By this I mean, rather than focusing on what was wrong, I focused on what was missing in my life and my relationship with Christ.

I was the client *again*. God's client. He was my Wonderful Counselor. I had never felt so naked, exposed, and vulnerable. That's what happens when your career, your dream becomes your identity.

I came face-to-face with my own brokenness, humanness, and shame. I felt exposed. I hadn't realized how much of my identity, worth, and value were neatly wrapped up in my performance and in what others thought about me. I used those months for more than just studying to retake the exam, and I immersed myself in God's Word, soul-searching, meditation, journaling, and spending time with mentors.

I realized I had been operating in pride, fear, and perfectionism. I had come to the realization that, as I was preparing for the exam the first time around, I couldn't absorb the material because it was being blocked by my performance anxiety. I didn't give myself ample time to prepare. I feared failing because I'd created an identity that was tied to my career and, even worse, my purpose. Yikes!

I specifically remember the night before my exam, a friend prayed what she felt were Jesus's words over me: *We have walked through many things together in the past few years, haven't we? So much learning in so little time. Don't be overwhelmed by it all. My grace is sufficient for you. Keep your eyes fixed on me and we will make miracles together.*

As I drove by myself to retake the exam, I noticed a difference in my heart. My identity was not at stake and I had a quiet confidence and inner peace. I realized the licensure exam was a logistical hurdle, and whatever the outcome, I had to trust God with my heart's desire to help hurting people.

Your salvation requires you to turn back to me
and stop your silly efforts to save yourselves.

Your strength will come from settling down
  in complete dependence on me. (ISA. 30:15 MSG)

I calmly and peacefully took the exam without crippling fear.
And this time I heard the proctor say, "Pass."

Perfectionism: A Self-Inflicted Cuckoo

As discussed in the previous chapter, perfectionism is a form of
fear. Specifically, a fear of man, a fear of failure, and a fear of rejection. Perfectionism is an obsessive preoccupation with performance, achievement, and appearance. Perfectionists look to
people and to work for their approval and validation. The source
of their worth and value is in what they do instead of who they are.

Perfectionism = Your Performance = Your Identity = Your Worth and Value

As with all self-inflicted cuckoos, perfectionism appears good
on the outside yet creates harm, because you gradually develop
an obsessive preoccupation that takes over your life. Self-inflicted
cuckoos are imposters disguised as something that will fulfill you
yet ultimately leave you feeling empty, lost, and lonely.

Unlike relationship cuckoos, with perfectionism cuckoos,
you are not feeding the insatiable appetite of a unhealthy person
but the insatiable appetite of your ego by searching for relief and
significance in unhealthy ways, such as being perfect.

The danger comes when the need to be perfect slowly
consumes your daily life and controls you. Like the host parent
of the cuckoo chick who becomes a slave to its ever-demanding,
never-satisfied demands, so it is with the perfectionism cuckoo,
because you are a slave to your own internal drives.

The perfectionism cuckoo begins as a passion and then slowly
grows into a crippling obsession that can become the sole source

of your identity, worth, and value. As a result, you get envious of others easily, resentful, competitive, or prideful, or you push yourself too hard, enduring dangerous levels of stress. Examples include being passionate about a project, a hobby, a ministry, or a career. The problem arises when your life becomes out of balance and your relationships, mental health, and physical health are affected. Your marriage suffers, you do not spend as much time with your children, you experience chronic fatigue, you are not sleeping well, you are struggling with bouts of depression, and you are anxious most of the time.

These are all signs you could have a perfectionism cuckoo in your nest even though you were originally passionate about what you are doing. We become driven by our performance instead of driven by our passions.

The Story of Megan: Exposing the Invisible Enemy of Perfectionism

Megan was a perfectionist and did not realize it. She left her corporate desk job to pursue her passion for traveling and helping people. She landed a job with an international human rights organization that rescues victims from violence in developing countries around the globe. She thoroughly enjoyed her new career and had the opportunity to travel the world and make a difference in the lives of women who were involved in sex trafficking.

She began to develop what she called a "food addiction" and wanted help to address this issue in counseling. She began to feel insecure about her appearance and body image because she had gained a significant amount of weight. Megan also felt ashamed that she would "eat too much" on the weekends after an intensive workweek.

Throughout our treatment together, it became apparent that she was suffering with chronic stress from her internal pressures of setting unrealistic expectations at work. Although Megan was passionate about her new career, she ignored her body's warning signs to slow down and take care of herself. This was quite easy for her to do, because many people tend to dismiss symptoms of chronic self-neglect when their work is meaningful and fulfilling, especially when they're helping others and saving lives.

Because of Megan's perfectionistic lifestyle, she needed an escape and a way to comfort herself, so she would binge eat on evenings and weekends. It was a pleasurable activity but provided only temporary relief. Her unaddressed stress was beginning to affect her health. It is common for people to self-medicate when they live under prolonged stress and perfectionism.

As Megan identified the perfectionism underlying what she labeled as her food addiction, she began to let go of her shame around binge eating. We addressed her deeper-rooted feelings of inadequacy. She learned to give herself permission to relax, have fun, and make it a priority to enjoy her life and relationships outside of work. She is no longer living as a perfectionism cuckoo and operates under the permission and freedom to just be and not always do.

The Internal Pressure of Perfectionism

I've discovered in my work that most of my clients are overachievers in all areas of their life and extremely hard on themselves. Many of those who struggle with perfectionism are hardworking and conscientious and have an intense inner drive to succeed in business, family matters, and ministry-related endeavors. They are often hugely competitive, high achieving, self-motivated, and their own worst critics. These very accomplished people do it all. They have successful businesses. They are small group leaders and church elders. They are involved in school functions, coach their children's sports teams, host community gatherings, attend events, lead committees, volunteer, and travel frequently. They are accustomed to putting a great deal of pressure on themselves and often feel as though they have not done enough.

This lifestyle and mindset are not sustainable, and eventually they turn to cuckoo-coping companions to find relief from their chronic stress and busyness. They are unaware of how to take care of themselves so they can recharge and heal.

Perfectionists are driven by internal pressures:

• Extremely high ideals and standards
• Unreasonable and unrealistically high expectations

In my practice, I've found the following outcomes of perfectionism: we lose the ability to be creative, we make poor decisions, we try to manipulate and control others for our own agenda, we cannot hear clearly from God and our intuitions. We are driven by our insecurities instead of our passions, we have little tolerance for people who make mistakes, and we cannot see the future from God's perspective. We lack wisdom because our reality is a distortion of the truth that we cannot fail. We live in pseudohope and call it faith when we are actually in fear. We get locked into a performance mentality, we accept quick fixes instead of long-term benefits, and we become stressed and too busy to enjoy life.

Additionally, people who struggle with perfectionism do not pause to celebrate their successes and quickly move to the next thing, they have difficulty receiving compliments, and they lack self-compassion. They have all-or-nothing thinking, do not know how to rest and have fun, and procrastinate due to fear of failure. They believe they are not allowed to make mistakes, are severely self-critical, and are susceptible to anxiety and depression.

I've discovered that perfectionism is rooted in shame. People who struggle with perfectionism are unconsciously avoiding deep-seated emotions of inferiority, inadequacy, and low self-esteem.

These feelings can stem from past pain, such as childhood trauma, an experience of public humiliation, or rejection issues in previous romantic relationships lacking unconditional love. To cope with the unresolved pain, they unknowingly develop an inner vow to prevent the suffering from reoccurring: "I will never be imperfect again."

Perfectionism is a lack of love for yourself.

Jealousy, Impatience, and Pride: The Fruit of Perfectionism

Toxic thinking patterns of perfectionism, such as pride, jealousy, envy, comparison, and impatience lead to self-sabotaging behavior. People who struggle with perfectionism do not wait well; they want immediate results. By not waiting well, they skip over the process from where they are to where they are going. Perfectionism adopts a mindset that is idealistic rather than realistic, how things should be instead of how things really are. The truth is that life is full of disappointment, it's messy, and we cannot control other people or circumstances.

Perfectionism leaves us wondering what life could be instead of taking it for what it is. Therefore, we miss opportunities to gain wisdom from God and insight from others, things we cannot see on our own. We bulldoze through important steps that are a necessary part of the process.

It is important to enjoy where you are now on the way to where you are going. Perfectionism does not allow that process; it jumps ahead to the result. We need the process; it is where we grow and mature.

Jealousy and envy are also fruits of perfectionism.

For where envy and self-seeking exist, confusion and every evil thing are there. But the wisdom that is from above is first pure, then peaceable, gentle, willing to yield, full of mercy and good fruits. (JAMES 3:16–17)

When we are envious and jealous of others, we see their success as a threat, and we can even raise the insecurities and mistakes in others, secretly hoping they fail or quit. We are unable to celebrate the victories of other people, people start to avoid us, we gradually become the victim and blame others for our mistakes, and we become self-absorbed and entitled.

We want to feel more powerful, popular, and talented than them. Jealousy and envy can lead us to finding ways to discredit others by exposing their weaknesses, gossiping, and trying to stir up a group of people to agree with us and tear down the other person.

Comparison is rooted in jealousy. Comparison steals our joy. Comparison sounds like "I wish I looked like him/her" or "I wish I had as many followers as they do" or "I wish I could do what they do." Comparison leaves no room for individuality and eventually thwarts a person's purpose. You are the only one who can tell your story and share your experiences.

Partnering with perfectionism will take us down a path of unnecessary suffering, leaving us bitter, unfilled, lonely, and disappointed.

The Fear of Man: Who Are *They*?

Perfectionism is rooted in fear. The fear of what other people think. It is the fear of man.

> *The fear of man brings a snare, but whoever trusts in the LORD shall be safe.* (PROV. 29:25)

People with perfectionism struggle with what other people think. They obsess over it. They build their lives around it. What will they think if "I cancelled Bible study this week," or "I can't do the car pool," or "I don't host the holidays this year," or "I took a season off coaching soccer," or "I step down from the PTA," or "I don't accept the promotion at work," or "I travel less frequently," or "I stop working weekends in order to spend time with my family."

I ask my clients, "Who are *they*?"

Do you realize you are letting the fear of what they think of you control your life? Every time you are tempted to worry about what they think, tell yourself, "Who cares!" I guarantee they are not thinking about you or caring as much as you do. We are trying to prove something based on our own insecurities and projecting it onto the cumulative *they*.

This toxic thinking pattern of what they think becomes a cuckoo. I encourage you to put the focus back on who you are, what you think, and what you want. Stop trying to be everything to everyone; that only creates suffering for you.

Perhaps you started a business or a ministry, and instead of enjoying the process of finding your unique voice and vision, you are constantly scrolling through social media and comparing yourself to others, wondering, *What will they think of my brand?* Or perhaps you have an accomplishment to celebrate in your business, and your joy is stolen because you feel as if your work is not good enough or big enough. You think to yourself, *If I can just get more blog subscribers. Start a podcast. A YouTube channel. Be the keynote speaker. Make a short film. Establish paid partnerships. A larger social media following. Write a best-selling book. Publish a magazine. Then I'll have succeeded!* Bigger does not mean better, especially if you lose yourself, including the things and people that are most important to you in the process.

It is not about building your brand, platform, or audience.

The truth is, those things might be your dream or your calling, but the real beauty is touching the hearts and minds of others, helping them in some way that also brings you joy and gives your life meaning. When you are driven by the fear of man, you strive for more and you lose touch with the people who are already in your life, perhaps within the four walls of your own home.

Fulfilling your dream is not about doing it perfectly and reaching your own unrealistic expectations. Ask yourself, "What brought me to want to do this ministry, career, or project in the first place?" Be honest. Are you consumed with what others think? Have you lost your desire in order to reach a few more?

Perfectionism creates much suffering and is a perversion of our God-given purpose and passions. Resist the compulsion to build an empire, be the number-one thought leader and top expert in your industry, or be the best of the best in order to be successful and happy.

The distinction is this: you should do what you do for God, not for them. What would happen if you stopped listening to their voices of what they think and paid attention to your own inner genius? To the voice of your Creator?

Choosing Passion over Obsession

Your career, ministry, or project is not the cuckoo; the cuckoo is your perfectionism around those things, and that is sabotaging. You might not need to get rid of those things, but you do need to kick the cuckoo of perfectionism out of your nest.

Perfectionism takes something you were once passionate about and turns it into an obsession, which takes the joy right out of it. The things you once loved to do become one more burden. Rather than it being life giving, it becomes overwhelming. You move from a passionate place to a joyless, powerless place. "I can succeed only when I'm the best." This perfectionistic belief blocks you from the thing you want to do and really enjoy doing. The lie wrapped into perfectionism turns passions you once enjoyed into chores.

Be true to yourself about what makes you happy and make choices from that place. The problem with perfectionism is that what really makes us happy does not line up with the image we have in our head of what we think our life should be like. If you truly want to be happy and not perfect, begin to change your image so you can change your life.

Take the time to heal from the wounds and face the fears that are manifesting in perfectionism and crippling your life. When is enough, enough? Make a choice today to redefine what success means to you and how you can be fulfilled in the here and now. Adopt an abundance mindset that includes success but also includes balance, healthy rest, and peace of mind.

Perfectionism holds the mindset that you must do *all* things perfectly at the same time. Just because you are gifted at so many things does not mean you can do them all.

As I have put this new perspective into practice in my own life, I have realized these opportunities come in small moments throughout each day. The choices I make add up to a lifestyle of passion instead of stress. For example, one afternoon, on my break between clients, I was in the middle of writing up my session notes, and I had a desire to go for a walk and watch the changing leaves. I initially brushed it off, "I really need to get these notes done so I don't have to stay late tonight." I chose the walk instead. I did not want to miss a present moment of happiness over doing the next best thing, falsely believing it would reduce my stress. What I needed was an autumn walk.

The Journey Out of Perfectionism into Victory

I can honestly say, with full confidence, that I am glad I failed that exam the first time around. There was a greater purpose to be discovered, and it redefined victory in my life. The truths I learned and the healing I received during those four months reconnected me with my humanness. When the perfectionism cuckoo tries to invade my nest from day to day, I kick it right out! If you are going to be a person of passion and purpose, you must face head-on your fears and the hidden heart issues underlying your perfectionism.

Perfectionism can rear its ugly head and make you realize your emotional capacity to deal with failure or disappointment was not as strong as you thought it was. Seeing "Fail" on my exam sheet revealed that reality for me. The process entails unexpected challenges, heartbreaks, and missed opportunities. We may even ask God what's going on. Allow the process to bring us to a place of healing, where we are no longer bound by perfectionism. God's intention is to free us; we just may not expect the painful realities we encounter on the journey.

To be a person of passion rather than a person of perfection, you need to have been in a situation where you experienced failure and where doors were closed in your face. Will you escape and give up trying or will you allow yourself to be confined to whatever limitation you perceive you are in and for a greater purpose you cannot yet see?

The surefire indication you are about to come into a season of passion is that you have been through a season of painful setbacks. Victorious people are not perfect people. Victorious people embrace the process, the mess, and the chaos. In fact, they welcome it because they want to learn more than they want to win. Victorious people do not resist reality; they face it head on. There are two realms of victory over perfectionism:

1. Being OK with failing.
2. Gaining greater insight into yourself, God, and others whom you did not know before.

Knowing who we are and whose we are come together to a place where perfectionism loses power.

I'll Be Happy Now

So many of my patients say, "I'll be happy when..." This tells me they are not happy now and have not yet embraced the art of enjoying life in the present moment. Their perfectionism cuckoo is demanding their attention.

Stop waiting for Friday, for summer, for vacation, for a promotion, for fame, for someone to fall in love with you, for a perfect marriage, for children, or for life. Overcoming perfectionism is achieved when you stop striving for it and make the most of the moment you are in now. If you keep living for tomorrow, you will eventually become jealous, resentful, discontented, anxious, depressed, and disappointed. Perfectionism will drive you to make a decision that will only end up hurting you down the road or, worse, you will miss out on God's best because you didn't trust his timing.

"Rest in the LORD, and wait patiently for Him; do not fret because of him who prospers in his way.... Cease from anger, and forsake wrath; do not fret—it only causes harm" (Ps. 37:7–8). The believer who waits patiently for God's perfect timing has nothing to be jealous of or afraid of. You don't need to be envious of those who are married or have a better job or fear you will never have the desires of your heart.

No person and nothing can bring you fulfillment, and you do not want either to do so! Certain people, jobs, and opportunities come into our life, but they are not designed to complete us, fill us up, or make our world. That is a dangerous thing to ask of a relationship or a career.

Freedom from perfectionism comes from being content and satisfied with yourself and from marveling at the precious gifts of everyday life. Therefore, when a thing your heart desires comes to pass, it is simply an added blessing and not the source of your identity, worth, or happiness.

For me, it's this moment, sitting on my patio and watching a storm roll in while I'm enjoying a cup of tea and listening to the symphony of birds in my backyard, instead of thinking, *I'll be happy when this book is published.*

If we wait for the life we want so we can be happy, we lose the life we have now. Rather than saying, "I'll be happy when . . . ," make the choice, "I'll be happy now."

A Real Rest

My clients who struggle with perfectionism take responsibility to extremes and take life too seriously, forgetting to play and have fun. We have an epidemic of perfectionism in our society today. Being average is somehow seen as settling or not doing our best. This leads to an identity crisis because people do not truly know who they are when they base their worth and value on what they do, what they look like, whom they know, what they know, or what they own.

Part of why people feel empty and stressed is they do not realize they are feeding a perfectionism cuckoo. They do not realize it's OK to pause. To take a break. To fall apart. To stop. To get counseling. To have fun. To rest. To let go.

This standard is tremendously difficult to achieve and can lead to buried anger. Overcoming perfectionism is learning how to parent yourself in gentler, kinder, loving ways than perhaps you experienced as a child. Accept God's grace to cover your mistakes and accept his unconditional love that is not dependent on your performance.

Are you tired? Worn out? Burned out on religion? Come to me. Get away with me and you'll recover your life. I'll show you how to take a real rest. Walk with me and work with me— watch how I do it. Learn the unforced rhythms of grace. I won't lay anything heavy or ill-fitting on you. Keep company with me and you'll learn to live freely and lightly. (MATT. 11:28–30 MSG)

CHAPTER 8

WHEN YOU BECOME A CUCKOO

Making Yourself a Project to Fix

---

*It is well to remember from time to time that
nothing that is worth knowing can be taught.*
—Oscar Wilde

Fix Me! Fix Me!
One of the most toxic relationships we endure is the relationship we have with ourselves. The most common yet subtle cuckoo behavior I witness my clients suffer from is through the defense mechanism of "projectizing," a term I coined, which is a deeper and more dangerous form of perfectionism.

Projectizing: Making oneself a project that needs to be fixed.

When we make ourselves a project, we disconnect from our true self because we do not know who we are or what we want, need, and feel. We are trying to fix ourselves instead. The defense mechanism of projectizing shows up in obsessively trying to fix ourselves and results in self-hatred and self-attack. Projectizing is rooted in shame. I realize self-hatred might seem like a strong word, but we must be honest with ourselves because if we truly loved ourselves, we wouldn't treat ourselves as a project that needs to be fixed.

The word *self-hatred* is distinct from a common phrase such as "I don't like my body." Self-hatred for being who you are embodies intense feelings of shame that are deeply entrenched and extremely painful. We are essentially being mean or cruel to ourselves.

Self-hatred takes on the form of projectizing, which is the need to make oneself a project to fix rather than seeing oneself as a person in pain deserving love and compassion. Essentially, you attack yourself for things that are beyond your control, because you intrinsically believe you are flawed.

As mentioned in chapter 5, "What Feeds a Cuckoo?," strongholds consist of defense mechanisms that are the lies we tell ourselves to avoid pain and block out the truth. Defense mechanisms hold us captive and keep us stuck in a cycle of suffering.

With projectizing we believe the lie that if we fix ourselves, we will be OK. In reality, we are feeding the shame cuckoo.

Jesus commands us to love our neighbors as ourselves, so it's biblical and apparent that we are to love ourselves. How can you love your neighbor if you don't love yourself? You might feel the pressure to fix them also and think you are helping them. Loving yourself means you show compassion, care, listen, and feel.

Imagine a loved one saying to you, "I've been feeling anxious lately and I can't sleep at night. I'm really struggling. I dread waking up in the morning, and I don't know how I'm going to make it through the day. I feel off. This has never happened to me before. I'm usually such a joyful person."

Would you respond, "You need to fix that" and have absolutely no emotion toward that person whatsoever? Would you only entertain an intellectual dialogue with them? I doubt it. Yet that is often how we treat ourselves.

A single woman desiring to be married is told she is too picky and not doing her part, so she feels shame that her singleness is her fault. Therefore, she is tempted to compromise her values because she falsely believes they are too rigid, and she ends up marrying someone she doesn't truly love. Or she spends an inordinate amount of time on dating websites and exhausts herself dating every man who shows an interest in her when she could be enjoying her life more fully. The reality is that she is single because she has not yet met a man she truly loves. Period. The truth is this: she is a strong woman who sticks to her values, and she is patient, confident, and content within herself.

But before she could receive these truths and begin the healing process, she had to face her pain and her feelings of anger, sadness, and fear that she was avoiding. Weekends were especially painful for her, especially after church on Sundays, when she heard the fun plans of how a couple of friends were spending the remainder of the day together. She longed for companionship. She was lonely.

Through her counseling sessions she learned there was more to her singleness that was causing her so much suffering. It was that she felt shame about her loneliness and her need to fix her singleness. During her treatment we discovered, at a deeper level, she felt intense regret for past relational mistakes and believed it was her fault that she was single. Therefore, she feared feeling her painful emotions and buried them as a result. This kept her stuck in a continuous cycle of suffering.

Once she was introduced to the truth and allowed herself to experience her anger and sadness surrounding her singleness, she learned not to fear those lonely moments during the weekends. Instead of projectizing her singleness and seeing herself as a broken person who needed to be fixed, she allowed the waves of sadness to pass through her and had compassion for herself and reached out to a friend or God for comfort.

Toward the end of our treatment together, she said, "It's amazing to me how simple—not easy—it is to sit with my loneliness. Yes, it is painful, but it does pass and I am OK! I'm incredibly grateful we identified the real enemy of projectizing so I no longer have to go through these tormenting and exhausting roller-coaster rides and mental Hula-Hoops trying to figure it all out. Now I can get back to living my life! I believe the right person will come along at the right time. After all, God knows my heart and I trust him, not just with my future husband but with my moments of loneliness."

All in all, her cuckoo was not the fact that she was single; it was believing it was her fault and therefore exhausting herself to fix it.

At the close of her session, she said, "I have never heard of the defense mechanism of projectizing before. My other therapists have never used the word with me. This is incredibly eye-opening and life-changing to be able to name this. I've struggled with making myself a project to fix all my life and never knew what it was. What freedom!"

Trying to Remove Your Cuckoo Makes You a Cuckoo!

On their first visit, many clients share with me the reason they are seeking counseling, such as anxiety, depression, and relationship issues. Clients who are unconsciously suffering from projectizing sit tensely on the edge of the sofa, determined to fix themselves. They are highly intelligent, motivated, and successful people. Often they hold back tears. They see feelings as a nuisance or an inconvenience to solving their problems.

They want tools so they can be fixed. They are impatient and in a hurry to fix the problem. They want things to go back to the way they were before they were struggling so they can be "happy or normal again." They do not see the connection between their suffering and frantically wanting to fix themselves. They are unaware of past and present underlying pains in their life and how these are affecting their current issues.

The cuckoo becomes you because you develop an insatiable need to make yourself better. This need, however, is never satisfied, because you will never have a pain-free or problem-free life. Your need to fix yourself every time a problem arises will overwhelm you, consuming your emotional energy and thought life. Instead of enjoying a life of purpose, fixing yourself becomes your purpose.

These clients desperately want to know things and how to be fixed at the cost of being known as a person. This tendency to fix oneself is a cuckoo in and of itself. Freedom from their issues entails doing the necessary work by facing the reality of their deep-seated pain so healing can take place. Many people unknowingly live out this cuckoo compulsion to fix themselves for most of their life.

We discussed the fear cuckoo in chapter 6 and found that control is rooted in fear, and one way control can show up is through an obsessive need to know. This toxic thinking pattern becomes an illness of introspection because we are scrutinizing ourselves, and we get stuck in paralysis by analysis. The more people try to understand and analyze themselves, the farther away the answer is and the more anxious they become.

Clients who struggle with projectizing always ask, "How do I fix this?" or "Why do I do this?" They say, "I just want to know why, so I can fix it." Understanding why we do the things we do is important; however, in these cases, the healing process it takes to get there is hijacked by their need to know right away. As previously stated, *knowledge in and of itself does not bring freedom.* Healing begins with facing your pain. Your pain contains truth, and the truth will set you free.

Once my clients are aware they are projectizing, they ask, "So how can I fix that?" We have a good laugh because they realize they are making their defense mechanism of fixing themselves a project to fix too! Their laughing shows progress because they are learning all the ways they try to projectize themselves every time a new problem emerges.

The following are signs of projectizing leading to suffering:
- Regretting the past or fearing the future
- Rooted in shame: "It must be my fault" and "I must have done something wrong"
- Mental torment and obsessively overthinking
- *Why* questions driven by desperation to solve the issue
- What-if statements driven by anxiety
- Isolating and oppressive
- Where Satan resides and feeds us lies
- Toxic symptoms (for example, depression, anxiety, stress, addictive behaviors) manifest and create suffering

The following are signs of overcoming projectizing, which lead to freedom:

- Accept reality: operate in the present moment
- Rooted in self-compassion
- Share your story: you have a capacity to receive comfort from others and you know you are not alone
- Experience painful emotions instead of avoiding them.
- Embrace your authentic self so healing can occur
- Ability to receive God's truth to dispel the lies
- Confidence to cope with challenging circumstances and difficult relationships in life
- Freedom from suffering

What my clients are experiencing alongside their projectizing defense is fear. They are afraid of feeling their pain and not having an answer so the pain goes away. What they do not realize is that making themselves a project to fix *is* causing them tremendous pain.

Their issues appear so big and scary because they feel this responsibility to fix it, which feels lonely and impossible to heal on their own. They seek to control by projectizing themselves and removing their heart and emotions from the equation.

For that reason, they want to have an intellectual conversation in therapy. They love homework and they want tools. I work with them so they understand what projectizing is and how the way they are thinking is complicated and chaotic because they are attacking themselves.

Projectizing deepens our suffering from already difficult situations and relationships. We want to fix it instead of facing it and feeling it. Those struggling with making themselves a project to fix feel a tremendous burden of what to do with the pain itself. The burden of responsibility to fix their pain is what they are avoiding, because it is mentally tormenting and isolating—as cuckoos are. This is due to the thought life and emotional energy needed for finding a reason why and then fixing it, alone.

I've discovered this defense of projectizing occurs beyond our conscious awareness and often develops in childhood, whether it involves rejection, abuse, neglect, or finding no validation or comfort in pain from our caregivers. As a result, we develop an unconscious vow that all pain is our fault. We believe at some very deep level we must have done something wrong, which is why making ourselves a project to fix is ultimately rooted in shame.

Many clients come to me after receiving no help or relief from previous counseling experiences. They have gained a plethora of tools but continue to remain stuck. Unfortunately, many therapists do not realize there is a strong defense of projectizing that is operating beneath the surface of the client's presenting problems, such as depression and anxiety.

When I Became a Cuckoo

I went through a season where I experienced migraines. I was confused why I had them because everything else in my life felt normal and fine.

I reached out to my doctor, who prescribed medication for my migraines. The migraines = always occurred in the early morning, so after I took the meds, they were gone after a couple of hours of lying in bed. Then I could go into the office to counsel. This pattern happened on and off for about eight months. I spent an inordinate amount of time, money, emotional energy, and thinking trying to figure out why and how I had developed these migraines.

I conducted a great deal of research on migraines. As a result, I scheduled an appointment with my primary care physician, met with a neurologist, did a sleep study, had an MRI, met with my dentist, saw an orthodontist, and started seeing a chiropractor to figure out the cause of my migraines. All of my results came back as normal. I was completely fine, and, in fact, very healthy, but I was frustrated.

There must be a reason! I was scared. I feared the migraines would never go away or that eventually they would worsen and affect my counseling practice and my life. What if my migraines worsened so I couldn't meet with clients? What if I couldn't pay my bills? In reality, this never was the case; it was my anxiety speaking. In addition to the anxiety, I felt ashamed. Somehow I falsely believed these migraines were my fault, so I had to fix them and find a reason. I was embarrassed to tell people I had them because I felt I had done something wrong. I was suffering.

A couple of months later, I was at church and bumped into one of the pastors there. She asked how I was doing and I explained I was having a problem with migraines. She sat me down and said, "Let's pray about this and see what Father God has to say."

As she prayed over me, she saw a vision of God turning on a faucet, which represented my emotions, which I had turned off while I was experiencing the migraines. That resonated deeply with me, and I told her, with tears streaming down my cheek, that I was angry with myself for having migraines. Sounds silly, but that is what I was feeling.

She said, "I feel you need to ask your body for forgiveness." That was the last thing I expected her to say! It felt odd and awkward, but I trusted her. She led me through a prayer, and I asked my body for forgiveness for being so mean and cruel to it, for judging it, punishing it, and being angry with it for the pain I was experiencing and for trying to control it. My migraines ceased completely and I've never had one since!

After that miraculous day, I developed an intense sadness. As I sat with that emotion and processed it, I realized it was associated with how I treated myself during the migraine months. I grieved over the way I treated myself. I was operating in the defense of projectizing—attacking myself. This shame manifested in expending so much time and energy trying to find a reason for my migraines instead of being compassionate and loving during a painful time in my life.

I created unnecessary suffering by being cruel and mean to myself. I judged myself for having migraines. I treated my body as if it was a machine or a robot that wasn't working properly and I wanted to fix it. Beneath the surface I was sad. Instead of feeling my sadness, I developed anxiety, which fueled my need to know why, because if I knew why, I could stop the pain. But instead of stopping the pain of my migraines, I wanted to stop the shame of believing they were my fault, that I had done something wrong, and I feared they would never go away.

I realize now, looking back at all my research, doctor appointments, time, and money, that everything was being fueled by fear in an attempt to control my pain. Control is always rooted in fear, and I was operating under a fear of pain. For me, pain equated to shame. I had failed. And it was my fault.

Additionally, for me the pain equated to feeling responsible. I felt a heavy, oppressive, mentally tormenting, and exhausting burden to fix it. It was isolating and lonely. So pain in this case created much anxiety for me due to this false pressure I was placing on myself.

For those reasons, it was not the actual pain of the migraine that was the issue; it was both the shame and the burden of trying to fix it that was the issue (the cuckoo) and the real source of my pain.

I developed this mindset due to my painful childhood; it was an all-too-familiar pattern that was occurring unconsciously beneath the surface of my migraines. It was not due to having unhealed issues; it was simply an old pattern trying to subtly manifest itself in a new way. Anytime I experienced emotional or physical abuse as a child, I was ashamed because I was told I did something wrong, even though I didn't, or I wasn't told anything at all and was punished for no logical reason.

I learned a valuable truth through this experience about my fear of pain and how it was causing me tremendous, unnecessary suffering. Being cut off from my emotions when I experienced pain that I did not understand was my pattern. This pattern caused me to ignore and dismiss my body, not have compassion on myself but rather try to force it to stop hurting.

Releasing my sadness was healing and freeing for me because it was a moment of beautiful conviction. Experiencing the reality of my emotion of sadness opened the door for truth to enter, to be comforted by God, and to hear him speak to my heart. *I never wanted to be mean or cruel to myself again when I was truly hurting. Instead of demanding an answer or a reason, I will choose love rather than making myself a project to fix, and I will nurture myself, believing the truth that the problem is not my fault.*

The most interesting truth of all was recognizing the reality that was actually occurring during those months of migraines. When I felt a migraine coming on, I would take my medication and rest in bed, and within a couple of hours it was gone and I was quickly back on my feet. All of the fears and what-if statements of not being able to counsel my clients or pay my bills one day because I feared the migraines would never go away was not my reality.

The truth that led to my freedom was that I was OK and my life was not disrupted. The suffering I put myself through was the result of:

- Blocking out my reality and my emotional pain via the defense of projectizing.
- I lacked compassion and couldn't give myself permission to have some type of physical pain that most of the population has experienced at some point in their life.
- I was no exception and it was not my fault.

Essentially, my need to know why and to fix my migraines became a cuckoo that consumed my thought life, exhausted me emotionally, stole my joy and peace, and created shame.

It was this experience that led me to create the term *projectizing* as a defense mechanism in treating my clients so I could put a name to what was creating so much suffering for so many. The defense of projectizing is the most common yet most deceptive of all the defense mechanisms I witness in counseling. We have enough cuckoos in our life to deal with already; let's not become our own cuckoo!

CHAPTER 9

CUCKOO COUNSEL

Who Hurts You and Who Can Help You

When someone shows you who they
are, believe them the first time.
—Maya Angelou

NOW THAT WE HAVE IDENTIFIED WHAT OR WHO IS YOUR cuckoo, whether it be an unhealthy relationship or a self-in-flicted cuckoo like perfectionism, you might be wondering, *Who is the right person to help me?* You do not have to know the answers to all the questions flowing through your mind (that is the role of a professional expert to assist you), but you must begin the process by asking for help so you are not alone.

As a clinician, based on more than a decade of experience counseling people who have a cuckoo in their life, it saddens my heart to state the reality that so many people who provide counsel (professional therapists, ministry leaders, and pastors) provide cuckoo counsel. By that I mean, rather than helping people, their counsel inflicts harm.

This chapter addresses the following issues based on my experience of treating cuckoo-counsel-inflicted clients:

- What makes a therapist a good therapist? How do we define a healthy counseling relationship?
- Do I stay or leave the counseling relationship?
- What does the counseling process entail?
- What do you say to the person in your cuckoo relationship about counseling? Do you ask them to join you? Do you tell them you are going?
- How do you identify the cuckoo's toxic behavior in a counseling session?
- Is my counselor a cuckoo counsel? How do I identify the counselor's cuckoo behavior?

What Makes a Therapist a Good Therapist?
How Do We Define a Healthy Counseling Relationship?

Many of my clients seek counseling after having been in therapy for years and suffering without experiencing significant symptoms of relief and without lasting healing after multiple therapists have failed. After a few sessions with me, they say, "I've felt a freedom here that I never experienced in three years of counseling with my other therapists after just three sessions with you! How do you do that?"

My response is simple: "I'm not trying to fix you."

So what makes a therapist a *good* therapist? A good therapist has gained innate wisdom from the pains of their own life that can be gained in no other way, but there is more to it than that. To fully answer this question, I need to clarify the purpose of therapy. A therapeutic relationship cannot be purely a method, a technique, a regimen, or something done to us. Something must happen *through* us. As we discussed in chapter 8, "When You Become a Cuckoo: Making Yourself a Project to Fix," you do not need to be fixed. You are not a problem to solve or a project; you are a person. The purpose of therapy is to help you, not fix you.

A good therapist does not simply discuss our thinking patterns, because therapy is not a head-to-head relationship or simply an intellectual conversation where the client does all the talking and the therapist does all the listening. Therapy requires a working relationship of mutual engagement between the client and the counselor.

A good therapist does not rely on knowledge alone, because awareness and understanding in and of itself is from the head, which will not heal the deep pain in our hearts. It is not an intellectual knowing that sets us free; healing comes from experiential, intimate knowing. Head knowledge can never be a substitute for relationship. I invite my clients into a relationship, which is the foundation for successful therapy. This is how lasting healing occurs.

The Purpose of Therapy

Symptoms such as anxiety, depression, stress, and relationship difficulties are what bring my clients into therapy. Many of their symptoms are rooted in the ways they have learned to avoid the truth: the truth of who they are, who others are, and who God is. Avoiding truth will never bring freedom; it will only bring suffering. Beneath a client's suffering are the lies they are believing and the emotions they are burying. A counselor helps us to see those lies that are invisible to us and the suffering they inflict. Then we can face the truths we have been avoiding, the truths that bring freedom.

By bringing these emotions to the surface so healing can occur and by exposing the lies to truth, my clients embrace the reality of their authentic selves. They begin to take the steps to confidently face their cuckoos. I work closely with my clients and take a very active role in addressing how they are stuck and suffering that is thwarting their purpose so they can live an abundant, meaningful life.

The reason I pursued my purpose as a counselor is because of my own experience of healing through counseling. People helped me face my pain in a safe and compassionate environment. It was the truth I learned during that season of counseling that set me free and brought tremendous healing. Because of my painful childhood I needed someone to sit with me while I sat with myself; I was used to enduring and carrying my pain alone.

Counseling is a relationship, not a formula or a technique. How can it be a technique when we're dealing with the heart and soul of another person? When I counsel my clients, we do not dialogue about their circumstances. I access their deep, innermost emotions and desires. As a counselor, I do not relate to my clients' symptoms or their diagnosis or their personality disorder. There is a person beneath those issues with a story of personal pain.

What is the purpose of therapy? Truth. And if it does not lead to freedom, it's not truth. How do I know this? Jesus said so:

Then you will know the truth, and the truth
will set you free. (JOHN 8:32 NIV)

We learn the truth in therapy. We learn the truth by embracing it in the reality of the present moment. My clients experience issues such as anxiety, depression, chronic stress, and relationship problems. These issues are opportunities for them to know the truth. I invite them to come out of suffering through the lies they tell themselves and the defenses they use that block out truth. Therefore, they come out of hiding from others, from God, and from themselves. They not only discover who they are but they can begin to walk into it and the truth it reveals, the truth that sets them free.

Will the Cuckoo in My Life Ever Change and Get Better?

The two most common questions my clients ask in therapy when they are in a cuckoo relationship are "Will the person in my life ever change, heal, or get better?" and "Should I stay or leave the relationship?" I address the answers to these questions so they are aware of any cuckoo counseling that does not align with the truth.

As I mentioned in chapter 2, "Stuck in Cuckoo Land," my response to the first question is for them to stop waiting for people to change and change yourself instead.

I do not disregard the fact that the unhealthy people who hurt you can change if they are willing to do the work, but the client must exert their own will in this process and the cuckoo must want help. The cuckoo might say they really want to change, but time will tell if their actions correspond to their words and they change their behavior. I advise my clients not to wait around if this does not happen, because they will be living in denial and false hope, which breeds deeper pain and suffering.

Hope deferred makes the heart sick. (PROV. 13:12)

People hope that the person in their cuckoo relationship will change at their desired time and in a certain way, and when that does not happen, their hope is delayed or postponed to some future time. Expectations are created, and they place their hope in the person changing when there is no change occurring. One of the major themes of this book is that *we suffer when we avoid truth, when we avoid reality.*

The reality is that we have been protecting ourselves from seeing the truth that the cuckoo will not change, even for us, no matter how much we have done to help them. Therefore, we suffer by being disappointed and disheartened, heartsick. We begin to believe we are not worth it. We feel rejected. We create defenses. "Maybe their behavior is not so bad . . ." We gradually become weary, impatient, depressed, weak, unable to stand strong. We become dependent on the cuckoo dynamic changing rather than changing ourselves and surrendering the cuckoo to God. You can never take the place of the Holy Spirit's conviction in someone else's life. You can only focus on your healing journey.

Letting go of expectation does not mean you lose hope or faith; it means you are protecting yourself and using wisdom by no longer setting yourself up for heartsickness and suffering. You will most likely have to go through this painful (but necessary) reality check, a grieving process, a loss of expectations, and put the focus off your cuckoo's behavior and back onto yourself. You have a choice to stay a victim to waiting and suffering or begin a new process that leads to freedom.

Do not remember the former things,
Nor consider the things of old.
Behold, I will do a new thing,
Now it shall spring forth;
Shall you not know it?
I will even make a road in the wilderness
And rivers in the desert. (ISA. 43:18–19)

Take a moment and ask yourself, *Am I willing to let God do a new thing in my life? Will I choose to* know *it? Can I place my hope in God instead of placing my hope in the other person changing?*

Should I Stay or Should I Go?

Now that you have identified that you are in a cuckoo relationship, you might be wondering, *Do I stay in the relationship or leave the relationship?* The answer is neither straightforward nor black and white. It is complex and nuanced. Many of my clients do not know what to do, and they become stuck in the land of indecision. My goal is to help them make the decision to stay or leave, but not from a place of being stuck.

Assigning Meaning: False Beliefs Around Staying or Leaving. It is important to note that assigning meaning to your decision to stay or leave or allowing someone else to do so is harmful. Placing assumptions on such a life-changing decision can create shame, doubt, and confusion. Some believe that leaving the relationship is the healthier choice to make or the stronger choice to make. The same could be said about staying. Staying means you have no self-respect or means you are weak. But all of these responses are unhealthy. They are false beliefs, false judgments. They oversimplify very complicated issues.

Every person is different. Each cuckoo relational dynamic is different. Labeling a person's decision to stay or go as unhealthy

or healthy, strong or weak is destructive and untrue. The decision to stay or leave can be made in unhealthy ways. Based on the
available research in the fields of trauma, attachment studies, and
neuroscience, these decisions are not simple because there are
complex systems in place stemming from childhood even.

Obsessive Overthinking Keeps Us Stuck. For my clients,
thinking about the answer to the staying-or-leaving question becomes all-consuming, emotionally overwhelming,
and mentally tormenting. This is because they are obsessing
mentally in their effort to figure it out. In addition to an already
painful relationship where a cuckoo dynamic is present, there
is an underlying layer of suffering in thinking about whether to
stay or go.

This defense mechanism is our mind's way of keeping us
preoccupied. The toxic thinking pattern keeps us stuck. It
is paralysis by analysis. We become stuck (paralyzed) with
indecision because of our constant overanalyzing. Obsessing
in your mind to figure out whether to stay or go prevents
you from making the decision to stay or go. You are living in
your head rather than living in your behavior. Our obsessive
thinking is distracting us and keeping us busy; therefore, we
falsely believe we are doing something. Obsessing is not doing,
and it is blocking us from doing, from staying or going.

Essentially, we are thinking instead of doing. Our behavior
will expose the cuckoo dynamics and help us determine what
is happening in our relationships rather than feeling stuck in
a tormenting mental bubble. Obsessive overthinking is also a
form of projectizing, making yourself a project to fix rather
than focusing your attention on the relationship and the other
person involved. You become the cuckoo when you are frantically fixating on the stay-or-go question. You are feeding your
own insatiable appetite of needing an immediate answer and

inhibiting yourself from making the decision to stay or go from a healthy place.

The Fear Cuckoo Rears Its Ugly Head. After meeting with countless clients who are stuck, I've discovered that fear is the driving factor in their place of suffering with indecision. The primary battle is with fear of uncertainty, fear of the unknown, and fear of abandonment. This is due to the enormous emotional, spiritual, financial, and relational implications that are painful and scary. When thinking about leaving a cuckoo relationship, they face new and different challenges, such as how their decision will impact their family and children, career, and living situation.

They are afraid of losing the relationship. They are afraid the other person is not willing to do the necessary work to change. That is a very scary reality to face. As a result, they become stuck, obsessively thinking about all these dynamics instead of taking action because of fear. What will happen if I set a boundary or stand my ground or say no or lose the relationship? Being stuck in your head about this decision is a way to avoid such big, scary, and hard questions.

Do the Work: How, Not What. Rather than focusing your attention on *what* to do, stay or leave, it is important to focus on *how* you make the decision. The how consists of the behavioral steps you have been applying (as discussed in chapter 2), which are setting boundaries and using your voice effectively when dealing with your cuckoo relationship. The how is the doing, the what is the thinking. If you do not apply those behaviors to your cuckoo relationship, you will remain stuck. Doing the work of applying those behaviors will guide you toward finding out if you should stay or go.

It is not about *what* decision you are making; it's about the process, the steps you take of *how* you arrive at a decision to stay or go and *how* you do it. Then you have your answer. If the other person in your cuckoo relationship continues to not honor your boundaries and continues to hurt you, you can say, "You have crossed my boundary of _____ " or "You continue to hurt me after I've asked you not to _____ " or "You are still repeatedly doing _____ after I have told you no" or "If you do this behavior again, then I need you to move out" or "I cannot be in a relationship where you continue hurt me. That is not acceptable for me" or "This is my boundary, so if you do that again, I need to separate."

Furthermore, remember to stop doing their work for them and to stop carrying the emotional weight of the relationship. Stop allowing them to monopolize your time and watch your life revolve around their insatiable demands. If you continue to give and they continue to take with no reciprocation, that tells you something. When your voice, feelings, and needs are not mutually acknowledged, that tells you something. If they continue to manipulate and control you, that tells you something. If they continue to lie to you and twist the truth, that tells you something.

When you set boundaries and use your voice effectively, you are going to find out what is true in the relationship. You will discover the reality of the other person's behavior, whether it is a romantic partner, friend, work associate, church leader, or family member. Then you will know whether they are changing or not.

Will they stop keeping secrets from you, neglecting parental duties, cheating, engaging in addictive behaviors, abusing you, or whatever it may be that is hurting you? When you take action steps, it will reveal to you the truth about them, and you can make your decision from a place of reality after having witnessed the facts. You have been focusing on your healing journey and doing the necessary work. Have they? Only you can answer that question based on their actions, their behaviors.

Suffering and Stuck to Focus and Freedom. It takes tremendous courage to do the *how* and to take these steps. You face your fears. Many people do not take the steps because they are afraid to find out the truth about the other person in their cuckoo relationship. They are ultimately afraid of losing the relationship. They are afraid the answer is going to be the painful answer of the person not being willing to do the work. This is a scary reality to accept. But you do not want to stay in a cuckoo relationship just out of fear of losing the relationship. If you are staying because you are afraid, your choice to stay is not a true choice. You are staying because you're stuck and suffering rather than out of the freedom to choose to be in a relationship with this person. That is not how you want to stay.

Leaving a relationship and creating a new life for yourself outside of the cuckoo dynamic must be based on your choice and knowing that you have taken these necessary steps to arrive at that decision as well as recognizing it is apparent the other person is not doing the necessary work to change, get help, or heal. You confidently believe that you are making the best choice for you instead of staying stuck in a cuckoo relationship where you are the only one doing the work, thus continuing the cycle of suffering.

Staying in a relationship must come from a deep inner knowing that you are making the best choice for you. You want to stay out of choice, knowing you could leave if you need to or want to, but you are staying because you choose to be with the person. You love the person, and they are also making the necessary changes to make the relationship work.

The ideal situation is one where we stay in our relationships and our relationships can be healthy. But not all relationships are healthy, and not all relationships are ones you can stay in. Both decisions to stay or leave can be made in unhealthy ways, and both can be made in healthy ways. Therefore, leaving is not always the better way and staying is not always the better way. You can stay from a healthy place or you can leave from a healthy place.

Remember, it is not about *what* decision you are making, it is about *how* you are making the decision and how you are walking it out. That is what influences whether the decision is a healthy decision that is best for you. How you do it is what is important.

As you grow and learn the truth, freedom emerges, and you can make major relational decisions from a place of empowerment and faith, not powerlessness and fear.

What Does the Counseling Process Entail?

If you find yourself feeling afraid and stuck over whether to stay or leave and are having difficulty setting boundaries, using your voice effectively, knowing your needs, feeling your feelings, that is what counseling is for. You do not have to figure this process out on your own. Accepting the truth that you cannot change the person in the cuckoo relationship, the first step is knowing the only person you can change is you.

It is important to recognize this at the beginning of your counseling process, and you will feel afraid, uncomfortable, and unsure. Do not be deceived into believing the changes you are making in your life are not good just because they do not *feel* good. Bringing awareness to your toxic relationships, thinking patterns, and behaviors exposes the underlying trauma and painful emotions you have buried for years because this is how you have developed your coping mechanisms to protect yourself. Just know that when you start *healing intensely*, you will feel intensely.

Having a safe person sit with you in your pain can help put words to what you have been experiencing, so you no longer feel alone and confused. Just remember, once you begin to do the work, you might feel worse before you feel better.

I experience this with my clients and remind them that feeling worse and uncomfortable means they are making progress. That is something to celebrate because healing is taking place and they are slowly becoming free and unstuck as they allow their hidden issues to come to the light so they can be dealt with.

I tell my clients there is no magic wand. A counselor is not a magician. People are often too afraid to look at their pain because they do not know how to deal with it. So many people do not understand their own suffering. They want their counselor to fix them or fix their cuckoo, and they get frustrated when they realize this is a process that takes time and hard work.

It Will Be Hard, but It Will Be the Right Kind of Hard

Counseling is a safe place to continue to work through the healing process and to go deep and do the necessary psychological and spiritual work as well as create a strategy to evict the cuckoo dynamics from your nest.

Due to being in an unhealthy cuckoo relationship that has left them with a painful and disorienting environment not grounded in reality, many of my clients do not see the truth about who they are. They have believed the lies of the cuckoo that they are unwell, weak, fragile, stupid, and at fault. I help my clients view themselves as strong, capable, wise, and resilient.

They feel out of control and controlled at the same time. They are exhausted emotionally and worn down mentally while they have been taking care of a cuckoo's needs and wants at the cost of their own. They have been deceived and manipulated into caring for this thing that does not belong in their nest, and they do not know what to do about it. They are too afraid to confront the cuckoo relationship, and thus unaware of their tremendous anger, among other emotions, that they have deeply buried. At times, I am the last in a long line of church leaders and counselors my clients have seen, and none have given them a voice or helped them to see the truth.

An expected part of the counseling process is the tendency to want to revert to old patterns of relating. "This is too hard. I'd rather just go back to the ways things were." This is a normal response once my clients reach a particular point in their therapy, which I call the Egyptian mindset.

After Moses brought the Israelites out of slavery toward the promised land, they had to endure forty years in the wilderness. The Israelites did not like the wilderness. It was intense, hard. They were unhappy, they complained, they were afraid, and they were sorry they had left Egypt. The Israelites were mad at God and mad at Moses, and although they were slaves and were treated terribly in Egypt, it was familiar because they still had food and water and knew what to expect every day.

During their time in the wilderness, God provided them with manna daily and they got tired of eating it. They wanted meat and they could not gather the manna for the next day or it would go bad, which made them feel afraid. They had to wait on God and trust him to provide for their daily needs. They had extreme diffi-culty placing their faith in God, Moses, or themselves to endure the journey to the promised land and often wondered if there really was a promised land.

The same principle applies as you embark on the journey to freedom in your counseling work. It is intense and can feel scary at times, especially as you begin to confront your cuckoo rela-tionship. Many clients leave counseling because they become too afraid. Often they resume their sessions when their suffering has overtaken them completely or they are in a state of crisis. Fear of rejection and losing the relationship with their cuckoo, whom they love, is normal and to be expected. Like the Israelites, it is easier to go back to what is familiar and comfortable, even though it is painful, rather than facing the fear of the unknown and the underlying pain that has been buried for so long. It takes courage and endurance, with the help of a counselor, to embrace their wilderness season.

Once my clients stay the course of their treatment, the relief of no longer feeling crazy, being stuck, and trying to fix themselves starts to bring healing. They begin to see their promised land, including the miraculous ways God stepped into their situation and parted the sea on their behalf when they least expected it, when they felt that had reached the end of themselves.

As the client, you must be willing to do the deep psychological work and recognize that the process takes time. Remember, you are doing the right kind of work because you have been doing the work for the cuckoo and neglecting yourself. Now you need to do the work for you.

What Is Right to Say to Your Cuckoo About Counseling?
Do You Ask Them to Join You?
Do You Tell Them You Are Going?

This question does not apply if you are dealing with a self-inflicted cuckoo. If you have a self-inflicted cuckoo, such as perfectionism, chronic stress, or addictive behaviors, you will need to pursue individual counseling. If you know of someone who is in a cuckoo relationship, this section will help you to help them.

It is important to engage the person in your relationship and invite (rather than demand or force) them to counseling for your benefit as well as theirs. You want to create a safe space and an opportunity with an objective third party, a knowledgeable expert and professional. Say to your partner, "I would like us to go to counseling. I have noticed that we have not been getting along." Use the phrase "I feel" as opposed to "You make me feel." Gently invite them into this new relationship by making it about the two of you together and enhancing your relationship and communication rather than criticizing, accusing, or pointing a finger at them.

If you feel stuck, I encourage you to ask your counselor, "Based on your experience dealing with _____ [describe your issue here], what do you suggest would be helpful to say to my partner because they are resistant to counseling?"

If your partner adamantly refuses to join you in counseling, then pursue individual counseling and keep your sessions private between you and your counselor. If your partner asks you what you are talking about with your counselor or if you are talking about them, gently let them know you are working on your issues and how you feel. Your counselor will help you address this situation as well and will guide you in the process of developing a strategy. The focus will be on what you are learning about yourself instead of attacking, defending, or placing blame onto your partner.

If you cannot have your partner in counseling (e.g., a boss or work colleague, family member, friend, or church leader), seek individual counseling and ask your counselor to help you deal with this cuckoo relationship.

Cuckoo Behavior in the Counseling Session

If your partner agrees and you begin counseling together, here are some warning signs of their cuckoo behavior that can occur during the sessions:

- They have a tendency to jump from counselor to counselor, firing the therapist if they do not agree with how things are going. (I've been fired because they do not want the truth to be exposed and to be held accountable.)

- Their behavior never changes. They know how to talk the talk.
- They are manipulating and deceiving the therapist with their charm and lies.
- They are not teachable and do not take responsibility for any of their behavior.
- They focus the sessions entirely on you and what you are doing wrong.
- They are unwilling to do their part to actively participate. You are the one doing all the counseling work.
- They act a completely different way in counseling than they do at home. They are performing and putting on a show for the counselor and seeking to win the counselor's approval.

Meanwhile, you, the client, feel just as disillusioned or more confused in counseling than you did before counseling. Your intuition is telling you something is not right about the counseling process and how your partner is operating.

Additionally, your partner should not use the counseling relationship with your therapist against you as a weapon at home by twisting the counselor's words to serve their own purposes. If they are in individual counseling and you are not a part of their therapy, do not let them manipulate their therapist's authority by saying, "My counselor told me you are wrong." This counselor may have never met you and is only hearing one side of the story. Finally, if the two of you are in therapy together, and they continue to have solo sessions without you present or separate conversations with your couple's counselor, this is a red flag, because every couple's counselor should have a no-secrets policy to prevent them from building an alliance with one client. In couple's counseling, the couple is considered the client.

Cuckoo Counsel

If it is apparent from your sessions that your counselor is not aware of any of the above warning signs regarding cuckoo-type behavior in the counseling session, and if it's brought to their attention and they disregard your concerns, you are experiencing cuckoo counsel. I would encourage you to use the above warning signs as a guide in your sessions. It is essential to pay attention to those warning signs and bring them to your counselor's attention. Let them know how your partner is behaving at home outside of the counseling sessions. This is especially true if the toxic patterns continue to repeat themselves, even though they are telling the therapist things are going well. If this is the case, I encourage you to initiate a private phone call or request a solo counseling session with your counselor. Let them know how you are feeling at this point in your treatment process.

Give your counselor an opportunity to address the problem. You might feel your counselor and your partner have partnered up and are building a case against you and creating an agenda that is not based in truth or reality. If you find after discussing these dynamics with your counselor that you cannot trust them, trust your intuition. It is OK to end therapy with your counselor. You can say to your counselor, "Thank you for taking the time to work with me, but I do not feel this is a good fit for me. Can you recommend other counselors who specialize in _____ [whatever the issue is]?"

It is important for you to do your research and find additional counseling options outside of your counselor's recommendations. Experiencing cuckoo counsel creates an unsafe environment because you are submitting yourself to their authority in the most vulnerable, emotionally intimate way and trusting their expertise. And if they abuse that authority, you are no longer safe under their counsel.

Below is a list of cuckoo counsel warning signs when your counselor is displaying unprofessional, harmful behavior in your therapy sessions:

- They accuse you of things that are not true, such as "I think you've been sexually abused" when this is not based in reality, and your behavior does not warrant such an accusation.
- They tell you that you need medication and label you with a false diagnosis. If this happens and you feel misdiagnosed, seek a second opinion from a trusted psychiatrist.
- They always agree with your partner and take their side. Therapy is not about agreement and taking sides; it is about relationship and collaboration.
- They excuse your partner's toxic behavior and do not hold them accountable.
- They defend your partner and find fault with you and place the blame solely on you.
- They brag on themselves and invalidate you as a result. "I've done this a long time." "I'm really good at this." "I know what I am doing." "I am the expert." A healthy counselor will never announce how good they are; they will just counsel you.
- They provide you with a personal opinion instead of professional counsel. "I would not want to be married to you." "You spend way too much time with your children." "Most couples have sex more often than you do."
- They are critical of your thoughts and emotions rather than providing a safe, inviting, and compassionate environment. A healthy therapist will address any pertinent issues in a way that you do not feel attacked or wrong for feeling a certain way.

- They isolate and control you by telling you not to engage with or talk to anyone else but them because they see it as a threat.
- You do not feel like a priority. You feel you are wasting their time. They are not truly listening to you. They constantly reschedule your appointments. They seem disinterested.
- They take what you say personally and tell you how they feel as a result. "This hurts me that you would say or feel _____."
- They give you bizarre homework assignments that make you feel uncomfortable and are not helpful in any way.
- They talk too much about themselves and their problems. They are too vulnerable and develop an inappropriate emotional intimacy with you as a result.

Never hesitate to tell your counselor exactly how you feel about them and how you feel the progress of your sessions is going. I frequently ask my clients, "How do you feel things are going in our time together thus far?" Clients might feel angry toward me over the course of our counseling relationship. This is normal and to be expected. I welcome all of their emotions because I want to be a safe person for them to be themselves and not fear my reactions and to learn to trust their own emotions. The counselor models for the client what a healthy relationship can look like outside of the counseling room.

You do not want your counselor, of all people, to jeopardize your healing process or create more suffering in your life in addition to an already painful cuckoo relationship.

Also note that your counselor does not know you better than you know yourself. Keep in mind that your counselor is not a psychic or a magician. They can only help you based on the information you provide about yourself. The more open, honest, and vulnerable you are, the more they can help you.

There is such a thing as too many voices. You do not need more complication or confusion, especially now that you are in therapy and under the counsel of an expert professional. Have a few select people whom you trust to bring into your journey. You can also speak to your counselor about how to engage these people in the process and what would be helpful.

I encourage you to not give up. There are wonderful, safe counselors out there who will be able to help you overcome your current traumatic experience in counseling. I have had so many clients with a long history of professional counselors, psychologists, and psychiatrists who have hurt them, and they are afraid of experiencing the same with me. The initial part of our time together is centered on bringing healing from their previous counseling experiences and building trust. The last thing you want is to feel crazier, more confused, and ashamed in therapy.

The next chapter, "The Religion Cuckoo: Twisters of God's Word," is dedicated to exposing religious and emotional abuse, specifically how church leaders and ministers can provide ill-advised, destructive counsel and label it as biblical. My clients and colleagues have urged me to write about this because they feel there is very little material available that addresses this issue. They feel strongly that fellow believers, friends, family, and churches, as well as other Christian counselors, need to be better informed.

CHAPTER 10

THE RELIGION CUCKOO

Twisters of God's Word

For pride is spiritual cancer: It eats up the very possibility of love, or contentment, or even common sense.
—C. S. LEWIS

A SILENT EPIDEMIC
The religion cuckoo is a silent yet serious epidemic in Christian evangelical churches and communities who provide ill-advised counsel and label it as biblical. Based on both my personal and professional experiences, church leaders provide cuckoo counsel by twisting the Word of God according to their own pain, hidden agendas, lack of knowledge, or from a place of fear in order to control. These can include pastors, ministers, priests, lay counselors, elders, mentors, or Bible study leaders.

This chapter discusses three primary ways in which I've found the religion cuckoo shows up for people: a law-based system of rules, dealing with mental illness, and emotional and religious abuse.

My Religion Cuckoo Story

As a child, I saw my parents' relationship embed into churches and religious systems where the religion cuckoo was prevalent, and this profoundly impacted their marriage and my life. It was damaging for both my parents and me.

As I mentioned at the beginning of chapter 1, a pivotal moment for me was when I learned about the moment my father threatened to kill himself if my mother left him. It would not have been out of character for my father to make this threat with no intention of making it a reality. My mother and I have not spoken often about that moment and the incredible mark it left on my humanity. I couldn't have expected what would have happened in that moment for my parents. My father must have been in a desperate state. He must have thought about finding any way out of his suffering, and of course I do not think he had any intention of killing himself.

As far as I can tell, my parents had spent many years in counseling, both pastorally and professionally, to improve their marriage. As a child and as a young woman, I had no context or understanding or experiential appreciation for what they must have gone through. I only remember feeling afraid.

Their divorce was the end of the end. The end of all the confusion, fear, misrepresentation, and fighting.

And I felt an overwhelming sense of relief.

As an adult and as a professional counselor myself, I understand these fears and complex emotions that show up in my clients' hearts. Although my parents' divorce was painful for many reasons, my mother, siblings, and I were able to feel safe in our home for the very first time because my father was no longer there. I was free from the continual cycle of trauma and suffering and living under a dark cloud of dread, shame, pain, and fear.

My own journey of healing coincided with my parents' divorce at a particularly difficult season of my life. I sat in the church waiting room, bouncing my leg up and down, trying to ignore my racing heart and sweaty palms. *What am I doing here? I should just leave. Wait, I am only meeting with the pastors as a favor to Mom. She knows I am hesitant to this idea because of past confusing church experiences, yet she said the pastors here are different. She feels supported and understood. After all, she has been through so much. The least I can do is this favor for her.*

I have to admit I was curious. Could these people really help me the way they helped my mother? My mind drifted back to painful memories related to both counseling and the church. *I can't wait to get out of here.* Before I could finish my thought, my name was called. I immediately felt my guard go up. What initially began as discussing my parents' divorce gradually became about me and my pain. After that, I sat on that sofa every week for a year.

I had grown accustomed to the way they brought Jesus into every conversation, as though he were another person in the room. They talked about him the way I would about a beloved father, a good friend, someone I really wanted to know.

The confusing and distant God I perceived at times during my painful childhood became my closest companion, Lord and Savior, caring Father, and the love of my life. In all my years at church, I had never experienced people with such contagious joy. Initially, it was something I couldn't identify, but I knew it was missing from my life, and I wanted to experience that deep-seated joy of the soul.

I began to feel the presence of Jesus in a real, tangible way. Although I had grown up in church and attended Christian schools, not once did I vividly experience a personal and intimate relationship with Jesus until that time in my life. I had only experienced religion, but from that moment forward I knew I belonged to him. I was his precious daughter, and this revelation was far more than the intellectual answers I was searching for. I had a relationship with the Creator of the universe. I had an encounter with the presence of Christ.

Needless to say, my hardened heart toward counseling, God, and the church began to soften, and my pain no longer held me captive. I had been set free from the religion cuckoo's snare.

Rules of Religion Over a Relationship with Jesus

Removing the religion cuckoo in my own life enabled me to have a relationship with Jesus, receive his grace, and know his compassion. The religion cuckoo elevates rules above relationship and uses the Scripture and the law to try and control people, eliminating the idea that we are a community learning from one another and evolving in our understanding.

Many evangelical churches and Christian communities operate in a religion void of a relationship with God, Jesus, and the Holy Spirit. People falsely believe their acceptance from God and their church leaders is based on their behavior, obedience, and performance. It has become a passion of mine to educate people on the difference between religion and relationship.

It is important to note that I am not inferring that all religion is a cuckoo. Religion can be a beautiful supplement to an authentic relationship with God. Many Christians embrace religion as an outward form of an inward faith (attending church services, praise and worship such as singing, communion, baptism, and prayer). But I am specifically critical of toxic religion as a cuckoo when it is used to control, generate fear and intimidation, and manipulate others.

There are some churches, Christian counselors, pastors, and people in ministry who counsel from a place of control rather than from a relational place of truly knowing the other person, their story, and their pain. They are more concerned with following the rules and being "right."

The religion cuckoo shows up as a modern-day Pharisee mindset and behavior patterns. During Jesus's ministry he regularly came up against the religious rulers of his day, the Pharisees and Sadducees. When Jesus was healing people and performing miracles, the Pharisees and Sadducees tried to oppose his anointing by reminding him that he was breaking the rules of the religious-based system of their day.

Their purpose was to accuse him and eventually destroy him, and they tried to accomplish this by holding him to their interpretation of God's law. The apostle John described this in his gospel: "For the law was given through Moses, but grace and truth came through Jesus Christ" (1:17).

For we are not wrestling with flesh and blood [contending only with physical opponents], but against the despotisms, against the powers, against [the master spirits who are] the world rulers

of this present darkness, against the spirit forces of wickedness
in the heavenly (supernatural) sphere. (Eph. 6:12 ampc)

Although we no longer have the physical presence of Pharisees and Sadducees, there is still a legalistic, accusatory, and religious spirit that operates in our churches and communities that seeks to render the body of Christ inactive and ineffective.

The kingdom of God is not a matter of talk but of living power (1 Cor. 4:20). Religion offers no power to heal and set free; there is no living proof of anything real. In this way, the religion cuckoo seeks to control people through fear by holding them to the law that governs their behavior. Essentially, they are all talk, following rules, and have no power to touch the hearts and lives of people.

The religion cuckoo is based on the law and creates suffering by robbing us of the freedom to live by the Spirit, abiding in our purpose, and experiencing a life of joy. The apostle Paul said that Jesus "has made us competent as ministers of a new covenant—not of the letter but of the Spirit; for the letter kills, but the Spirit gives life" (2 Cor. 3:6 niv).

The religion cuckoo is a performance-based system of rules adhering to a particular set of beliefs and practices. The religion cuckoo was invented for people to interpret for God what he meant to do rather than coming directly to him in relationship.

People long for what is real and authentic. Why adhere to a church or religious community that provides no hope, no experience, no transformation, and no real meaning to life? Jesus is after our hearts, not a system of man-made rules.

These people honor me with their lips, but their hearts
are far from me. They worship me in vain; their teachings
are merely human rules. (Matt. 15:8–9 niv)

The Pharisees had no understanding of the Father's heart. They loved the law more than they loved Jesus. Jesus's ministry came from a place of compassion. The religion cuckoo brings guilt and condemnation and the constant reminder that you are never good enough, followed by feelings of inadequacy.

Jesus said, "You search and investigate and pore over the Scriptures diligently, because you suppose and trust that you have eternal life through them. And these [very Scriptures] testify about Me! And still you are not willing [but refuse] to come to Me, so that you might have life" (John 5:39–40 AMPC).

Even Jesus differentiated between the Scriptures testifying *about* him and our willingness to come *to* him. How do we come to him? Through relationship. By being authentic and vulnerable, through revealing our pain, our brokenness, and our genuine emotions. Searching and investigating the Scriptures is necessary, as it provides us with truth and tells of God's character and nature.

The Holy Spirit illuminates the written Word and makes it come alive on the inside of us in the context of intimacy with Jesus. What are you looking for? Religion or relationship? Jesus shows us the way. He exposed the religion cuckoo in the Pharisees' and Sadducees' teachings while healing the brokenhearted and setting the captives free. Jesus was in the business of breaking the man-made rules of his day and following the purpose of his Father.

The religion cuckoo can manifest itself in many areas of life, such as in parenting, sexuality, and other places that are too big to discuss in this book. Instead, I am focused on how the religion cuckoo shows up in relationships by trying to control what happens in marriage and, specifically, regarding mental health issues, divorce, and emotional and spiritual abuse.

If you are single or in a committed romantic relationship, this chapter is significant for you by helping you to understand healthy marriages and how to deal with mental illness. This chapter also addresses the warning signs of when the church is providing ill-advised counsel and labeling it as biblical. This is especially important if you plan on getting married and there is a strong possibility the church will play a role in your premarital counseling.

The Emotionally and Religiously Abusive Marriage

Another way the religion cuckoo shows up in relationships is through emotional and religious abuse. Countless clients come to me after having seen numerous pastors, professional Christian therapists, and lay counselors, or they come to me referred by their pastor or church ministerial staff hoping I will fix the wife or husband and "heal their marriage."

What none of these counselors or ministers realizes is that one spouse is being emotionally and/or religiously abused. They are in an abusive relationship, and the ill-advised church counsel is actually feeding their cuckoo dynamic and deepening their suffering.

What Is Emotional Abuse?

In my counseling, I've observed that the evangelical church has been rather passive and quiet about acknowledging the reality and legitimacy of emotional abuse, especially in marital relationships. My goal is to advocate for these men and women who have been harmed, shamed, and neglected by their church leaders and religious communities.

Emotional abuse is a pattern of behavior in which one person attempts to control, intimidate, and manipulate another. Emotional abuse causes serious trauma and has a significant impact on a person's mental health. As with all cuckoos, my clients do not recognize this invisible enemy is right in front of them, because emotional abuse is not easily recognizable. Emotional abuse is a difficult form of abuse to detect because the harm being done is not physical. The wounds of emotional abuse are invisible. Many clients have said, "It would be easier if my partner would just hit me or cheat on me so at least I could point to that so people would understand my pain." This is because the church does not recognize the pain and harm of emotional abuse as being equally as devastating and harmful as physical abuse.

Emotionally abusive tactics include humiliating, belittling, verbally assaulting, name-calling, criticizing, and shaming. Emotional abusers attempt to isolate you from your friends and family. They can neglect you by purposely and vindictively withholding love and affection as a form of punishment. They can be extremely jealous and falsely accuse you of cheating. They constantly monitor your behavior: whom you go out with, where you go, how you dress, and how you spend money. They can threaten to leave you or abandon you or even threaten suicide if you do not act the way they want you to. They attempt to thwart your purpose, your professional goals, by instilling self-doubt. Ultimately, as with all cuckoo relationships, your life revolves around them, and pleasing them becomes your purpose.

The religion cuckoo pretends that emotional abuse is not valid. Its ill-advised counsel says you can leave someone only if your partner cheats on you or hits you, but they can emotionally abuse you until you are severely mentally ill. And even in cases of physical abuse, the religion cuckoo will encourage men and women to forgive and give more chances while the violence at home escalates. They do not realize the abuse is going to escalate without intervention. They believe the person should come in and get prayer and a scolding from the pastor or elder board and everything will be fine, and then they send the wife or husband and children back home to a spouse who is escalating the abusive behavior.

What Is Religious Abuse?

Religious abuse is one of those topics that is rarely discussed and often disregarded and avoided in the church. In our culture, *religious abuse* and *spiritual abuse* are often used interchangeably. Spiritual abuse occurs when another person tells you how to behave, what to believe, what to think, and how you should feel by exerting their power to control you. Ultimately your own thoughts, feelings, and beliefs are not permissible and you could be punished.

Spiritual abuse encompasses all religions and occurs across all populations. Spiritual abuse can take place in a variety of settings. It does not just happen in churches; it can happen in the workplace, in the home, and in school systems.

For this chapter I will be focusing on religious abuse, which is a form of spiritual abuse in the evangelical church, and how it shows up in marriage. Religious abuse occurs when a spouse or church leader uses God and Scripture (twisting God's Word) as a disciplinary tool or a weapon to control, intimidate, and manipulate another person.

Religious abuse happens when Scripture or beliefs are used to shame or humiliate you as well as coerce you into giving your time, energy, or money that you do not have or want to give "for the purpose of ministry" or "because God has called you to."

Religious abuse also entails spiritualizing another person's emotions by telling them their feelings are evil, sinful, or wrong. For example, if a partner is expressing anger toward the other partner in a healthy manner, they are told they have "a spirit of anger" and need prayer. Or a spouse tells their partner they are still having difficulty trusting them after having been lied to repeatedly, and they respond, "You need God to heal you of your distrust and bitterness. You still haven't forgiven me."

Religious abuse also happens when your church leaders or partner is using Scripture to control your finances, clothing, sexual intimacy, relationships, and important life decisions, such as where to live or whether or not to have children.

Under the toxic weight of the religion cuckoo, you lose yourself to another person who deceives, manipulates, and controls you for their own selfish agendas. Your own thoughts, feelings, and beliefs are dismissed or criticized if they do not benefit the other person or religious organization. The religion cuckoo trains a person to ignore his or her true self in exchange for their religious teachings and scriptural ideas. They want you to ignore your own inner, spiritual, moral compass. Eventually you lose the freedom to think for yourself.

The religion cuckoo operates under the lie that other people have the answers for you, and if you do not accept their beliefs or ideas, there will be terrible and very personal consequences. Anytime we are being disconnected from the conscious awareness of our inner-most being because we are being coerced by another, there is a religion cuckoo in our nest. We need to honor the deepest part of our spirit and soul as sacred and precious. Do not allow the religion cuckoo to smother and destroy your eggs. Protect them.

The Issue of Abuse and Divorce

When I meet with clients who are in an emotionally and religiously abusive marriage, I've discovered that when physical abuse or infidelity is not occurring, men and women receive cuckoo counsel from their church that divorce is not an option, because divorce is a sin and God hates divorce. These men and women are already suffering the pain of abuse, and now they also feel they are a sinner and disobedient to God if they leave their abusive spouse.

Rather than helping them deal with the emotional or religious abuse and even identify that abuse is happening in the relationship, they are told to try harder, fight for the marriage, work toward reconciliation, God can do miracles, stay in the marriage for the sake of the children, pray for healing or God's intervention, if you just do such and such your spouse will come around, he says he is willing to change, just give her more time to heal, or ask God to help you be patient. Meanwhile, the religion cuckoo ignores the traumatic experience of the partner being abused by their spouse.

The reality is that the spouse is in an abusive marriage, and the truth is that God hates abuse. Emotional and religious abuse *is* abuse. My clients have said, "My pastor believes divorce is only an option if physical abuse or infidelity is taking place in my marriage." Physical abuse is not worse than emotional abuse. *Abuse is abuse.* And infidelity and physical abuse does not trump emotional abuse in the case for divorce.

In these cases, the cuckoo idolizes the marriage unit and ignores the spouse and their experience of abuse. The lie is that God cares more about the marriage than the person and their suffering. The religion cuckoo uses the marriage as a weapon to control the person's decision to divorce an abusive spouse and therefore makes a mockery of marriage. Emotional and religious abuse is not God's intent for marriage. Marriage is a covenant and not an idol to elevate above painful realities occurring in the lives of each spouse. God does not manipulate us, as his children, into submission via control and fear.

In fact, I have found in working with clients that emotional abuse has a deeper psychological impact than physical abuse because it is an invisible wound. The lies, control, manipulation, and confusion involved in all three of these happen on a daily basis. Physical abuse, although extremely painful for obvious reasons, is recognizable, but this is not always true for emotional abuse, which is part of the suffering so many endure.

In my treatment of clients, I have observed that divorce most often happens when one or both spouses refuse to do the necessary work required to change their toxic behaviors. There is no better indicator of change and reality than time and action (behavior). If one spouse is emotionally and religiously abusing the other and will not admit it or seek help or change their behavior, they are not submitting to God's will for the covenant of marriage, and they are not loving their spouse the way Christ loved the church.

A Story of Emotional and Religious Abuse

Laura came to me hesitant and highly anxious for her first counseling session. She tensely sat on the sofa and explained that she had recently left her husband, Graham, the associate pastor of a large evangelical church, and she was staying with a friend.

She explained that she was overwhelmed with guilt and shame over her decision to leave her husband. Laura said it was the most difficult decision of her life. "I am a Christian woman leaving my husband," she cried. "I've learned at church all these years that God hates divorce, and that divorce is a sin."

In that initial session, I asked her to share with me why she had left, and she very timidly whispered, "I'm not being physically abused or anything, and as far as I know Graham has never been unfaithful, but I don't feel safe and neither do my children." I gently asked her to elaborate.

The church leadership became aware that she and Graham were having marriage issues. They instructed Graham to seek marriage counseling. Out of an obligation to his pastoral duties, he agreed. Laura and Graham began seeing a licensed marriage counselor. The counselor diagnosed Graham with narcissistic personality disorder and identified his behaviors toward Laura as abusive.

Laura said that during the therapy sessions Graham was quiet and agreeable, but when they returned home he was furious and told her that she had disrespected and humiliated him in front of the counselor because she lied. "I am a pastor! How do you think this makes me look?" He accused her of twisting the truth to make him look bad and said the counselor did not understand their "unique" situation. Graham ended therapy.

At church, Graham explained to the head pastor that he and Laura no longer needed counseling and that everything was fine. Laura was devastated as Graham's abuse continued to escalate at home. She felt trapped. After all, Graham was very well liked and respected in their church community. Laura had to keep everything about their life a secret, and from the outside it appeared as though they had the perfect family.

Laura's friend was relentless in getting her the help she deserved. It never occurred to Laura to seek counseling on her own until her friend recommended her to me. When she told Graham, he was concerned but told her to spend her sessions addressing the many unresolved issues from her past that were the cause of their marriage problems. He told her she was not trying hard enough or fighting to fix their marriage.

After listening to her painful and heart-wrenching story, it was apparent to me she had been emotionally and religiously abused. After she shared her story, I encouraged her to write down all the hurtful things Graham had ever said or done to her and their three children and to bring her list, however long or short it was, to our next session. I purposely did not share with her the clear signs of emotional and religious abuse. My hope was that the exercise would bring it to light and she could see it for herself, which would give her confidence and clarity.

During her next session, she read through her list as she relived all the horrific memories and experiences that occurred over many, many years. The emotional and religious abuse was like the death of a thousand cuts to her soul.

Tears streamed down her cheeks. She said, "I really felt like I was crazy all these years. Now I see the truth." That moment marked the beginning of her healing process and journey to freedom.

Mental Health Issues and Church Counsel

Part of the cuckoo counsel in churches is that they believe they are equipped to deal with these incredibly complex problems that people are dealing with when the church has zero clinical training on the brain, the nervous system, and the attachment system. Church leaders have no clinical, psychological, and professional education of how the human body and psychology works.

This is another religion cuckoo dynamic because the church leadership does not know anything about mental illness, but they pretend and operate as if they do. They try to use faith and prayer to deal with mental health issues. They wouldn't do that with cancer. They wouldn't do that with a broken leg. They wouldn't do that with diabetes. But for some reason, when it comes to mental, emotional, and relational issues, church leaders believe they know what to do and how to counsel people. They inappropriately use their spiritual and theological authority to deal with the most intimate and vulnerable issues of the heart and the soul.

There is a difference between inner healing, spiritual direction, and pastoral counseling and professional counseling regarding how to deal with relational, mental health, and emotional health issues. Using inner healing by bringing Jesus into traumatic or painful memories can be helpful to people, but these methods can take a person only so far. Essentially, they are addressing the spiritual component, not the psychological. These two are different things and they each have a role, but unfortunately the church keeps trying to do the psychological role.

As discussed in chapter 3, "The Cuckoo of Not Feeling Your Feelings," emotional work is an essential component in the healing process. I have discovered with my clients that they have been sent the message at church that they should fear or dismiss their emotions because emotions are negative, wrong, and even sinful.

Many religious and church leaders believe and teach that our emotions are irrelevant to our Christian life or perhaps an obstacle to our faith or that our emotions should be disciplined or controlled. The truth is that our emotions do not cause the problem; it is our defense mechanisms against feeling our feelings that trigger our pain. God created us biologically with emotions for a purpose. We cannot grow spiritually beyond our emotional immaturity, because we are stuck emotionally.

I do not recommend that people go to their church for counseling. Most pastors have had maybe a class or two in which a module addressed counseling. They have no clinical training on the neurobiological ramifications of trauma or addiction or mental illness and how that affects people.

I cannot emphasize this enough: *Do not seek the church for counseling.*

If you decide to involve your church in your relational issues or for premarital sessions as a requirement for a pastor to marry you, the final section in this chapter provides some warning signs and specific questions that need to be asked and answered. If you are reading this and you are already deeply involved in counseling with your church, ask if they have a professional counselor referral. If they do not, begin the process of researching and finding a professional counselor on your own.

A Story of Mental Illness in Marriage

Samuel was suffering in his emotionally abusive marriage for years. His wife was diagnosed with bipolar disorder, and she was no longer open to pursuing therapy as she did at the beginning of their marriage. She stopped counseling and would regularly go off her medication. She was unwilling to get help medically and psychologically. She emotionally neglected him, moved to a different bedroom, stopped having sex with him, and was not willing to do the necessary work to change.

Samuel and his wife spent many years under the counsel of their church leadership. The church denied and never addressed the severity of his wife's mental illness and how it impacted the marital relationship. The church leaders and lay counselors advised him to continue to pray for her healing. That is spiritualizing, not psychotherapy.

He came to his first counseling session with me, and I asked him what he wanted to work on in therapy. Samuel said, "I want to fix my marriage. Nothing seems to help and things are getting worse."

After sharing with me the context and background of his story and previous church counseling experiences, I asked, "How are you feeling?"

"I feel stuck. I'm feeling lost and confused. I don't know what to do about my marriage."

I responded, "That must be hard, yet those are all thoughts you shared with me; none of them is a feeling. Can you tell me how you are feeling right now?"

"I feel broken," he said while looking down at his shoes.

Here again he is sharing a thought and not a feeling. By disconnecting from his feelings, Samuel also disconnected from me. He saw himself as broken instead of his marriage as broken. "I realize you say you feel broken. Are you a broken person? Or is your marriage what is broken?" I asked.

He responded, "I've done everything I can to please her and help her. She didn't used to be this way. When we first got married, she really enjoyed my company. We had fun together. I don't know what I did wrong. I know she can be better."

I helped him understand that he was in denial. That he was lying to himself that his wife's issues were his fault. By embracing this lie, he is against the truth. The truth was that his wife did not want help, she did not want to change. Remember, our defense mechanisms, such as denial, are the lies we tell ourselves to avoid our painful emotions.

He was entertaining a fantasy of an imaginary wife who would love him, get help, move back into the bedroom, communicate with him, and be a happy family.

He did not want to feel the intense anger and sadness he was feeling. He did not want to accept the reality of the marriage he was in. He wanted to relate to his imaginary future happy marriage and share his testimony of redemption and healing that his church encouraged him to pray for.

I asked, "What are you feeling toward your wife?"

"I just don't understand why she won't get help. Why she stopped taking her meds. Why she won't come back to the bedroom. Why she won't talk to me anymore."

Again, he was thinking and not in touch with his feelings toward his wife. I shared, "You don't have to understand why she does those things for her to do them. It doesn't need to make sense to you for it to make sense to her. Whatever is happening does not need your understanding. It exists whether you understand it or not."

As his counselor, speaking the truth in therapy is not a lack of empathy or compassion. It frees people from their lies.

He responded, "I never thought about it like that. I just don't want to give up. I want this to work out. I'm a loyal person. I can't help it."

"Can we accept that you want this to work when she doesn't?" I asked.

A tinge of sadness came over him. "Well, I guess I just keep hoping things will change. I pray about it all the time."

"You mean you keep wishing *she* will change," I said.

By telling Samuel the truth, I reminded him of who he is, namely, the man he had neglected in order to please his wife.

"I guess so," he timidly said as he looked away from me.

"Seems like you keep hoping for a healthy wife who will accept help instead of a mentally ill wife who rejects treatment, who does not want help, and who is not willing to do the necessary work to change."

Samuel believed he was loyal to his wife, but in reality he had been loyal to his fantasy of her changing and choosing him.

I repeated the question. "How do you feel toward your wife?"

He paused and eventually answered, "I am angry with her. I am also angry at God."

I asked if he would like to spend some time looking at his anger. As a result, we were able to process his deep-seated feelings of anger that he had buried for so long.

He said, "I feel ashamed that I am not being loyal to my wife and my children by having a voice and stating my needs and boundaries."

Denying his reality by living in a fantasy of loyalty was the true source of his pain, blocking out truth and creating suffering. By avoiding his pain, he could not see the lies he believed: he was a failure as a husband, it was his fault, and he had not loved his wife enough. All of this had tortured him for years. And the truth was his wife had already left. She was the one who abandoned the marriage and gave up, not him.

I said, "It seems you take your anger toward your wife and direct it back on yourself, resulting in shame. You say you are stuck, but perhaps it is the lies you are believing of not being loyal that are keeping you stuck. In reality you are a loving and caring husband and father."

Tears began to pour down his cheeks and became deep sobs. "I guess I am afraid."

His breakdown revealed he was beginning to accept the reality. Although painful, our breakdowns of our lies and defense mechanisms lead us to a breakthrough of deeper truth. Truth brings freedom. It does not break us. It heals us even though it is scary.

"Hope deferred makes the heart sick" (Prov. 13:12). Samuel kept hoping his wife would change. He waited and waited and suffered and suffered. Later in therapy we discussed that for a decade he had waited for her to become someone else. The hard part was facing how she had rejected, neglected, and abandoned him for years and then blamed him. Thus, she had divorced him years before without his realizing it.

As Samuel waited for her to become better, healthy, and happy, he punished himself, believing he was broken, a failure, and yet his marriage lacked intimacy on every level. He called this loyalty. Now, he was learning to embrace the facts, the truth that she had left him many years ago.

Samuel began to take full responsibility for the life he created, even though it was a hard reality to face. The role of rescuer was easier, believing "I can be strong and do the work for the both of us." Although that sounds pure and righteous, Samuel became empty within his hopeful fantasy that he could fix his wife's mental illness. He lost himself and was not living in the truth. He was living in a cuckoo relationship under the church's ill-advised counsel, which labeled it as biblical.

Questions and Warning Signs

What should you do when you realize you're dealing with a religion cuckoo?

Speak with a trusted friend or family member about your emotionally or religiously abusive situation and pursue professional counseling. For the reasons mentioned above regarding mental health, do not go to your church for counseling. Furthermore, professional counselors abide by a code of ethics and licensing standards specifically designed to protect their clients from harm.

If you are thinking of joining a church or religious community or seeking professional counseling from a therapist who is a Christian or if you are in an abusive relationship and considering divorce because the abuse continues, the following are important questions to ask your counselor or church leadership before beginning a counseling relationship or becoming a member:

- What are your beliefs on emotional and religious abuse?
- Do you believe that emotional abuse and religious abuse are abuses?
- Do you believe that emotional and religious abuse are just as painful as physical abuse or being cheated on?
- Do you believe emotional abuse and religious abuse are grounds for divorce if my spouse is unwilling to change their behavior and continues to abuse me?
- Do you believe I am disobeying God, that I am a sinner if I consider divorcing my abusive spouse?
- Do you believe I can allow the Holy Spirit to speak to me, hear his voice, and trust my heart in this counseling process?
- Do you believe my emotions are created by God and are important and relevant to my spiritual life?
- Do you believe I have to submit to my spouse if my partner is emotionally or religiously abusing me?
- What does your counseling process entail? Are there certain truths or nonnegotiable beliefs I need to be aware of?

Here are some warning signs signaling that the church is providing ill-advised cuckoo counsel:

- The counsel you are receiving seems inconsistent with the character and nature of Jesus. For example, you feel shame or fear with your counselor. You are being told not to trust your emotions, to control them, and that they are sinful. You feel afraid to question your pastor or counselor and give your opinion.

- You feel the church has taken the side of your abusive spouse because they cannot see the reality of abuse. They insinuate your relationship with God is not as valid as theirs. They use their authority and Scripture as a weapon against you to intimidate you. You feel ashamed, as if you are doing something wrong, when you are not abiding by their rules or taking their advice.

- You are told you are not fighting hard enough, praying enough, or trusting God enough in the relationship when your partner's abusive behavior continues with no conse-quences. You are told that God is teaching you a lesson about patience and long-suffering rather than addressing your partner's abusive behavior.

- When expressing your desire to get a divorce, as painful as that may be, you are told that God hates divorce and you are a sinner, while they ignore the abusive behavior of your spouse. You feel as if you are acting in disobedience to God when you have a voice in the session, disagree, and do not do exactly what you are told.

- They tell you that you have "unhealed issues" and that you need to be healed when you are stating facts of the reality of your abusive situation. For example, you share your anger about an abusive comment your partner made, and you are told, "You have a spirit of anger. We need to heal you of that." You unexpectedly find yourself as part of an intervention and you are being coerced into a situation where you are outnumbered.

The therapeutic process can seem overwhelming. Take it one step at a time and do not go through it alone. There are trustworthy counselors who are experts in their field, and they will advocate for you and help to create an effective strategy for you to obtain healing and break free.

CHAPTER 11

A PROTECTION AGAINST CUCKOOS

The Gift of Anger

The greatest gift you ever give is your honest self.
—FRED ROGERS

HAVE DISCOVERED IN MY WORK WITH CLIENTS THAT ANGER IS one of the most misunderstood emotions. When anger is avoided, we can create corresponding symptoms of unnecessary suffering, and when we address our anger, we can use it as a protection against the cuckoos in our life.

Anger is an emotion that occurs automatically in our brain and in our body, which means it is part of how God created us. Biblically and spiritually speaking, many people mistakenly believe anger is a sin because they misunderstand what the apostle Paul meant when he wrote, "'Be angry, and do not sin': do not let the sun go down on your wrath" (Eph. 4:26). Paul was saying it is OK to be angry, just don't sin when you're angry. It is how we deal with our anger that makes the difference. Going to bed angry gives a foothold for anger to grow into bitterness, unforgiveness, and resentment if not dealt with in an appropriate, timely manner.

Anger is an emotion we experience toward someone or something that is meant to motivate us to action and is designed to be motioned through the body and be released. Although anger is often considered a negative emotion, it can be constructive in helping to clarify your needs and wants in a relationship, and it can also motivate you to find solutions to the problems that are troubling you and hindering you relationally and personally. This includes how to deal effectively with the cuckoos in our life by setting boundaries, knowing our needs, and having a voice. Anger is a key emotion in stopping the cycle of allowing our cuckoos to continually take advantage of us and manipulate us. In this way, anger can be a gift.

It is important to note that your anger can be a signal alerting you that there is a cuckoo in your life that you are not dealing with. Therefore anger serves to protect you.

Anger is a signal worth paying attention to. Our anger may be a message that we are not addressing a significant pain in our life. Perhaps you have become responsible for carrying the emotional weight of a relationship. Your anger may be sending you a message that something is not quite right. This is a common experience when a cuckoo is in your life that you have not yet identified. Perhaps you are being manipulated, deceived, and taken advantage of or your anger can be telling you that you are being harmed, that your rights are being violated, that your wants and needs are not being met.

Another sign of having a cuckoo is that your life revolves around them, and your feelings, voice, and needs are not being mutually acknowledged. You continually give and they continually take. Therefore, anger is a useful emotion to inform us that we are giving too much of ourselves to another, that the relationship is lopsided because we are doing all the work. Additionally, our heart's desires, purposes, values, and ambitions are being compromised in the relationship. Cuckoos are never satisfied, no matter how much you try to please them, so our anger may be telling us that we are giving more of ourselves and doing more than we can comfortably do.

Becoming aware of our emotions gives us a sense of our identity, and anger is an emotion that protects the core of who we are. Anger is an essential way we make sense of our relationships and allows us to know ourselves and be appropriately intimate with others who are safe and trustworthy. Anger mobilizes us to act in productive ways to pursue healthy, reciprocal relationships. This enables us to create room for our purpose in life to manifest, essentially our eggs to hatch, instead of being smothered by a cuckoo. When we avoid our anger, we lose this valuable information, and we become vulnerable to relational patterns with cuckoos.

Ways We Avoid Our Anger

Avoiding anger does not make it go away. We can ignore it, medicate it, or pretend it does not exist for days, even years at a time. But it will show up in some form, including depression, anxiety, illness, shame, self-hatred, unforgiveness, or even violence.

We avoid our anger when we suppress this emotion. Anger must be experienced and externalized (mobilizing us to action) and not internalized. It is important to note that internalizing does not mean processing; it means keeping your anger trapped inside you. When anger is internalized, you are like a sponge absorbing your anger. Anger directed at oneself can be a form of shame, believing the lie that we are at fault for something harmful that is being done to us. Essentially, we are punishing ourselves for another person's harmful behavior directed at us. Many of my clients unknowingly direct their anger toward themselves rather than the person they are angry with, which can result in the physical and emotional symptoms of anxiety and depression. Anxiety and depression are common in people who internalize or avoid the primary emotion of anger.

The most common reason we avoid anger is because we are afraid to express our anger. We learn unconscious ways to avoid our emotions because of past painful experiences. Therefore, we have learned to ignore, distrust, or withhold our anger. Perhaps when we were growing up, we were punished and/or neglected when we expressed anger rather than having a parent who created a safe place to validate and process our emotions willingly and openly. Or we may be in a relationship in which we have learned that expressing our anger leads to rejection, judgment, criticism, blaming, and shaming.

In my clinical practice, most of my clients do not seek counseling for anger management issues related to an inability to control their temper. Clients do not say, "I have unresolved anger" or "I am avoiding my deeper-seated anger toward my spouse for not spending time with me" or "I am anxious at work because of my buried anger toward my boss." Rather, they struggle with anxiety-related symptoms and tell me, "I feel stuck." Stuck is a sign to me that my clients have unexpressed anger due to unresolved pain or unmet needs and have anxiety related to an inability to express anger. Perhaps they are so overwhelmed by the needs and demands of the insatiable cuckoo in their life that they have buried their anger so deeply and now operate on autopilot. Many people feel trapped inside a cuckoo dynamic, whether it is an unhealthy relationship, career-related, church-related, or self-inflicted cuckoo such as perfectionism. They do not realize they are angry.

My goal is to help people identify and resolve their unaddressed anger. To keep a direct focus on their buried emotion of anger, I ask, "What is the feeling *toward* him/her for _____ [whatever the issue may be]" as opposed to general, open-ended questions, questions that require a yes-or-no answer, or a question about what they are thinking. We both know at this point in the treatment process what they are thinking and how they are behaving. By asking them the feelings question, I invite them into what they are feeling in the present moment toward the person who has hurt or upset them.

Although the question appears simple and straightforward, it is often met with avoidance, primarily through defense mechanisms. Clients' answers are typically marked by a rise in anxiety or an "I'm not sure" response.

Clients might respond by saying, "I feel sad," and they become weepy. In this situation, the sadness is not an emotion *toward* the person who hurt them; the sadness is a feeling they are experiencing and internalizing within themselves. Their sadness is a way to avoid the scary, uncomfortable emotion of anger. Many clients tell me they feel sad when they exhibit signs of anger. It is less scary in these moments to feel sadness than it is to feel anger.

Clients can also respond with toxic overthinking. They spiral off into a string of thoughts (instead of feelings), giving all sorts of intellectual reasons as to why they think the other person is behaving the way they do or describing how disappointed they are. They fall into a place of paralysis by analysis and become stressed and overwhelmed.

Regardless of their responses, I invite them back to their present feelings and what their body is experiencing in the present moment. They learn valuable information about the ways they unconsciously avoid their anger and how it is hurting them instead of helping them. Ultimately the goal is to break free and heal from painful relationships that are holding them captive, so they are no longer stuck and powerless.

At times we will uncover the client's anger toward me as part of the healing process, since the counseling relationship *is* a relationship, and often what they experience with me reflects how they experience relationships outside my office. They learn to externalize their anger honestly whether it be a yelling episode or sharing with me what they want to do to the person they are angry with, because they know our sessions are a safe place to freely express those emotions without a filter.

Internalizing anger and continually burying it over a prolonged period can manifest in outward ways. Anger can become excessive when it is expressed in unhealthy ways that are dangerous or harmful to them. Uncontrolled expressions of anger include hostility, aggression, abuse, or violence.

The following chart is a summary of the above ways I have witnessed countless clients avoid their anger by internalizing it and how it manifests in their life:

Which methods of internalizing your anger do you most relate to?

Next, take a moment and name the cuckoo in your life. Ask yourself, "How do I feel toward him/her for _____ [name the specific issues that have hurt or upset you]."

Allow yourself a moment to pause and get in touch with your anger.

How do you experience the emotion in your body?

Does anxiety, shame, weepiness, or overthinking show up? If so, that's an important realization! These are all signs that you are avoiding your anger. Notice which feelings come up when you feel angry. This realization is an important step.

Make the choice to stay in the moment and feel your anger.

While you are alone, as part of this exercise, speak to your cuckoo as if they are in the room, and tell them what you honestly feel, think, want, and need.

Call a trusted friend and tell them how you feel toward your cuckoo. The purpose of this exercise is for you to express your feelings of anger by releasing them.

Once we have addressed and processed our anger and identified the ways we can avoid it, the healthy, productive way to express anger is to set boundaries and have a voice (the specific steps were discussed in chapter 2, "Stuck in Cuckoo Land").

Externalizing Anger = Action
Having a Voice, Setting a Boundary, or Both!

Setting a boundary in relationships with friends, family, and colleagues and in ministry puts a limit on unacceptable behavior. Boundaries are personal guidelines you establish to identify safe and permissible ways for other people to treat you and to define how you will respond when those boundaries are crossed. Boundaries are formed around your personal values, morals, and beliefs, so they can include spiritual, mental, emotional, and physical needs.

Giving anger a voice means telling another person the truth about how you feel, what you think, what you want, what you need, sharing your opinion, and saying no. Many people were taught as they grew up that their needs were unworthy, so as an adult it is difficult for them to say what they need.

As you begin to clarify a more independent sense of self by setting boundaries and having a voice, feelings of anxiety, guilt, and false beliefs of selfishness tend to show up. If you are feeling guilty and selfish, you know you are on the right path.

The ability to freely express anger allows you to become more fully in charge of your life and to express yourself in constructive ways. Our anger can motivate us to say no to our cuckoos and the ways we've allowed them to take advantage of us, and it can help us to say yes to the needs and heart's desires of our true self.

We can also remove ourselves from the role of pleaser, fixer, or rescuer and stop chronically neglecting our needs. Remember, you cannot change another person; you only have the power to change yourself. The difficult choice is yours.

It is important to keep in mind as you begin to express your anger in healthy ways, some relationships might be lost as you go through these new changes in protecting yourself against cuckoo relationships. For this reason, being in touch with your anger can be scary and uncomfortable. You might want to fall back into old patterns of keeping your anger inside, which is a normal part of the healing process. Ultimately, rather than protecting the cuckoo in your life from your anger, you will start to protect yourself against their harmful behavior.

The Story of Julie: A Client Whose Anger Brought Clarity

Julie sat on my sofa stuck and confused. She expressed how she was introduced through a mutual friend at her church to a lovely man named Liam, whom she began dating. She shared how she was having an enjoyable time and was pleasantly surprised to discover that not only did they share their faith, which was extremely important to her, but his values and morals also matched her own in very specific ways. She said that he was an attorney and had also earned a doctorate in theology and volunteered in the prayer ministry at church. Julie very much enjoyed their intellectual, spiritual, and philosophical conversations. She was delighted because these qualities in a relationship were the innermost desires of her heart.

On the surface, Liam had everything she was looking for in a future husband. But she was acutely aware, each time they were together, that she felt no spark, no chemistry. Yet she continued to go on dates with him and hoped the chemistry would come. "I should just give it time," she rationalized.

Simultaneously, she began to develop underlying symptoms of anxiety. She experienced nausea, headaches, and difficulty concentrating, and she was not sleeping well at night. Each time she would describe her dates with Liam, she did not seem excited and spent more time trying to convince herself what a great man he was. When I brought this up, she said she felt a tinge of guilt about not being more excited about the relationship.

I came to realize in the session that the emotion hidden behind her anxiety was anger. When I asked her, "What do you want?" she responded, "I don't know, but I feel stuck and trapped." She felt as if she *had* to keep dating Liam, even though there was no chemistry on her end. After more work together. she discovered a lie that at a deep level she believed it was her fault that there was no chemistry, so she had to push herself to keep dating him until the chemistry came. After all, he appeared on the outside to be everything she was praying for and looking for in a potential spouse. She also spiritualized her emotions by saying she should be grateful for this relationship and asking if this was God's will for her. Therefore, she concluded she must be missing something or doing something wrong.

Additionally, the feeling that she was trapped was rooted in shame based on some history repeating itself from her abusive childhood. Because the abusive episodes inflicted on her by her father were unpredictable in nature, and he told her she'd done something wrong, Julie felt trapped. In between the abusive episodes she felt ashamed, believing it was her fault, and was trying to figure out how to prevent the next one from happening, what she did wrong, and how to fix it.

It was the same dialogue and pattern occurring with dating Liam. But as an adult, the reality was that Julie was not actually trapped. But her worry brain did not know the difference, because at some deep level it felt the same. It was not safe to feel the anger toward her father as a child for abusing her. In her relationship with Liam, the more she ignored her anger, the more anxious she became. Anxiety was symptomatic that something was wrong. She had internalized and absorbed her anger, which manifested in anxiety. As I mentioned earlier, anger is designed to be externalized, felt, and acted on as a protective mechanism by giving it a voice or setting a boundary.

Julie had learned to drown out her heart and intuition by coming up with reasons as to why there was no chemistry: "Maybe I am too picky or maybe my expectations are too high." "Maybe chemistry is not that important." "Maybe I was not ready to date." "Maybe my heart was not really open." The self-inflicted cuckoo of toxic overthinking was consuming her thought life and creating unnecessary suffering.

Throughout our sessions together, Julie realized that none of the above scenarios she had considered were true; they were based in shame and a fear of never finding a man she would want to marry. The reality was that she was very much open to dating. There was no block or issue hindering her. And she was certainly not expecting too much or being too picky. Her shame of feeling as if there was something wrong with her was directed toward what was missing in her relationship: chemistry, joy, excitement.

She was doubting herself and not acknowledging that she was wise, strong, and capable of making healthy choices based on her heart's desires, because she didn't trust them. She said, "I did not realize I was angry with Liam. Even though our lack of chemistry is not his fault, I'm still angry with him." After acknowledging her anger toward Liam, she was able to identify things he had said to her that irritated her and she had brushed off as no big deal. "I am also angry with God and was feeling ashamed about that. Why can't he answer my prayers?"

Julie was able to see the connection between her feeling of anger and believing she was stuck and trapped. She was also able to see the link between feeling anxious (headaches, nausea, and so forth) and saying what she really wanted. Pointing out her guilt over not having chemistry with Liam led her to identify her true desires. She confidently said, "I know what I want now. I want to end the relationship with Liam."

Julie stated how freeing it was once she made the decision to call Liam and thank him for the lovely dates and let him know that she did not feel any chemistry and wished him luck in his future dating endeavors. The truth and wisdom from acknowledging and expressing her anger through having a voice with Liam set her free from her suffering related to her anxiety, toxic overthinking, and shame. Julie had gained the tools to identify her anger by not turning in on herself and trying to figure out what she did wrong. She chose to live in the reality of the present moment and not a possible future chemistry.

During Julie's final session, she explained how her previous therapist was not able to help her identify her anger. She said the cognitive behavioral therapy sessions used by this therapist only provided a rational, conscious approach to her dating dilemma with Liam. She said the emotional processing she experienced in our sessions was just as important as identifying her cognitive distortions. In fact, it helped her understand them even more. Her healing went far beyond the Liam issue that brought her into therapy in the first place. She gained a deeper understanding of herself that she could carry with her throughout all the areas of her life. Ultimately, addressing Julie's underlying anger gave her valuable information about herself that will serve as a protection from entering unhealthy cuckoo relationships in the future.

Where your anger resides, there you will discover buried wounds that need to be healed and unresolved grief that needs to be addressed.

CHAPTER 12

THE ANTIDOTE TO CUCKOOS

Discovering Your Purpose

*"Life is never made unbearable by circumstances,
but only by lack of meaning and purpose."*
—VIKTOR FRANKL

IF CUCKOOS ARE THE CULPRIT, PURPOSE IS THE ANTIDOTE.

Focus on Your Eggs

In addition to creating pain in your life, cuckoos suffocate your passions and hijack your identity, and eventually you lose yourself. This is because you chronically neglect your own needs, wants, and desires to please and take care of them. Essentially, the cuckoos in your life destroy your purpose. The unhealthy relationships and self-sabotaging behaviors become your purpose because your focus is entirely on them. It is time to focus on your eggs (your purpose) that were suffocated by the cuckoo and not able to come to life.

The number-one indicator you have a cuckoo in your nest is that you have lost purpose. You might have been unaware you had a cuckoo in front of you, but you are aware that your eggs were unable to hatch.

Thus far this book has given you the tools necessary to identify and deal with the cuckoos in your nest, but what now? How do we take our identity and purpose back? How do we nurture our own eggs? These last three chapters of this book not only answer this question but will show you how your pain is the platform for your purpose to manifest and for your eggs to hatch.

Our cuckoo-coping companions—work, sex, food, alcohol, and the internet—distract us from our purpose and create suffering. Or we end up feeding the insatiable appetite of our own egos as we strive to be perfect and be the best. As a result, our cuckoos grow bigger and bigger and our purpose becomes smaller and smaller.

We spend an inordinate amount of time and energy feeding our cuckoo's needs and wants instead of cultivating our own passions and desires. If you do not stop feeding your cuckoo, you will stop nurturing your purpose, your eggs. Consequently, like the host's eggs, our purpose never births and eventually dies. Or we feel guilty and selfish about pursuing our purpose because we have unhealthy people in our life who tell us we are selfish or are abandoning them to pursue the desires of our heart.

Your cuckoos become your purpose. Cuckoos are purpose takers and eventually kill your spirit, so you end up feeling defeated and lost and never discover your true identity, namely, who you are and what you want.

Cuckoos try to prevent you from living the abundant life Jesus died to give you. Cuckoos, like thieves, come to steal, kill, and destroy your nest of eggs.

> *The thief does not come except to steal, and to kill, and to destroy. I have come that they may have life, and that they may have it more abundantly.* (JOHN 10:10)

Learning to Know You

Up to this point in the book, you have learned how to recognize the invisible enemy in your life, your cuckoo, and how to deal with them, which are the first steps to breaking free. Now, the final step is learning to know you.

Your eggs are a part of you. They are your signature. Your eggs are what you release into the world. Only you can hatch them. Your eggs represent your unique purpose in life.

An interesting fact about cuckoos is that not all hosts are naive to their sneaky patterns. Some "females go so far as to lay eggs with unique spots, squiggles, and colors that serve as a sort of signature. If they spot a forgery [i.e., the cuckoo egg], they'll push the egg overboard, not incubate it, or abandon the nest altogether."[22] Your signature is your purpose. It is what makes you unique and sets you apart.

Biologists and researchers who study parasitic birds, such as cuckoos, have discovered one of the cuckoo's hosts. "The tawny-flanked prinia lays probably the most diverse eggs of any bird species. They're works of art, but this diversity also carries great information content about their individual identity. They can be blue, red, white, or olive-green, and overlaid with a huge variety of markings including spots, blotches, scribbles and networks of filigree. Each female's eggs look unique, like a human signature. So that makes it extremely hard for the cuckoo finch to match any one host female's eggs well enough to trick her into accepting it as one of her own."[23]

The key to having diverse eggs is to be uniquely you. You are a work of art. Beautifully and wonderfully made. Your story and who you are intimidates cuckoos. Even biologists support this concept and state that "writing signatures on your eggs is a very good defense against parasitism."[24] Parasites use and take advantage of their host with no useful return.

This chapter is dedicated to showing you the secret of how to make your signature eggs, your purpose, unique so your nest is not susceptible to cuckoos.

How do you do this? Through knowing and discovering your purpose.

What Is Purpose?

Purpose whispers to you in the deep recesses of your inner being. Purpose has always been there, but only you can discover it. It calls to you like a long-lost friend. You can ignore that still, small voice that gnaws at you, but the gentle tapping on your soul will continue to show up in unexpected ways and unexpected places. Discovering your purpose requires you to take a look inside your story and to search the depths of your heart.

Your purpose is directly tied to your story, which includes your pain. Your purpose gives meaning to the suffering created by the cuckoo in your life. It is not an easy or simple process to move beyond a life once consumed by a cuckoo to living a life of freedom to pursue the things that create a deep-seated joy of the soul. It takes courage to pursue your purpose.

More specifically, purpose entails your essence as a person, that is, who you are and what you want, operating from your places of passion, your irreplaceable role in the lives of others, your story, and the specific talents, gifts, and strengths that are unique to you.

Your purpose is knowing and understanding why you were born. Your purpose is God's autograph on your heart's desires. It is your calling, as orchestrated by God, that only you can fulfill. It is your testimony of how your places of pain transform into your place of power.

It is important to note that your purpose can be more than just one thing. It integrates well with your past and is factored into the equation of your future. Furthermore, purpose does not always equate to an occupation, dream, or career. A meaningful life generally includes an occupation. This occupation must be considered your purpose if it is to truly satisfy your soul.

Here are several key principles regarding your purpose:

- It is God's thumbprint on your life. The desires of your heart are in its manifestation.
- It seems impossible. Do not miss out because you think it cannot be done.
- It is bigger than you. Without the help of God and others, you cannot accomplish it on your own.
- It requires faith in God. It seems too crazy to speak aloud. It feels too good to be true.
- It requires patience. Enjoy the journey and do not focus on the destination.

- It feels familiar. It is already a gift in you that other people are drawn to and recognize.
- It doesn't matter what happened in your past. God has already factored it into the equation of your life.

The Distinction Between Dream and Purpose

So many people, authors, speakers, and influencers share messages geared toward how to discover your dream. The message of "living your dream" is a bit of a cliché you hear quite often. But I believe there is a distinction between dream and purpose. A dream is a position or a career or a relationship or a status or a ministry or a business. Dreams might be a portion of your purpose in manifestation. Your purpose, however, includes your dream, but purpose is a place of abiding, not a thing to accomplish.

In summary:

Purpose = Your Dream + Your Vision + Your Passion + Your Heart's Desires + God's Calling on Your Life + Your Story + Your Pain

Purpose = A Permanent Dwelling Place and Deep-Seated Joy of the Soul

The majority of people lose their purpose because their dream (career, relationship, status, wealth, ministry, business) becomes their purpose. Their dream becomes their identity. This is a dangerous place to live and makes your nest more attractive to cuckoos.

Your Dream Is Situational but Your Purpose Is Relational

Similarly, happiness is situational (dependent on people and circumstances). Joy is relational. Your dream might make you happy, but it is not your true identity, your purpose. Perhaps you are not currently in a cuckoo relationship; maybe you are even living your dream in terms of your career and your ministry, or your dream of being married and becoming a parent has come to fruition. These are all wonderful things, but you cannot get your identity from those roles or relationships, important as they are.

You may be living your dream, but there may be other areas of your life and relationships that are lacking, out of balance, or suffering significantly. Examples include your marriage, you experience chronic stress and fatigue, you rarely see your children, your coworkers avoid you, your spouse is more like a roommate, your closest friends and family feel neglected, you don't have fun anymore, you're anxious most of the time, you never feel truly rested, or you no longer feel God's presence or hear his voice.

The above are all signs that your dream could be making your nest vulnerable to cuckoos because, yes, you are living your dream but you do not have purpose. Purpose is a deep-seated joy of the soul, where your life is balanced and your relationships and body benefit, not suffer, as a result.

As is the case with cuckoos, the process is deceptive and subtle, so most people unknowingly allow their dreams to become their identity. This is because they have given too much power and attention to one area of their life. Although their dream is a good thing, their life has gotten out of balance or their most intimate relationships have been neglected.

Using Dreams to Avoid Reality

A major theme of this book is that *we suffer when we avoid truth, reality.* I have found in my work that many people can use their dreams to avoid the reality of painful circumstances, disappointments, heartbreaks, and failures. Their dreams end up attracting cuckoos, such as an affair, poor business decisions, and addictions. They avoid the reality of their pain and hope their dream is the fix, and they end up with more cuckoos in their nest.

If you do not know who you are and whose you are as a child of God, you will not fully experience your dreams, the desires of your heart, and the abundant life. You will jump from dream to dream, event to event, person to person, relationship to relationship and never be fully satisfied. Or the other areas of your life will suffer significantly, become out of balance, and take a back seat. If your dream is being a wife/husband or a mother/father and you obtain that dream, what if your spouse cheats? What if they die unexpectedly or you lose a child or your ministry falls apart or you lose your job?

Most people's dreams are unconsciously or consciously created as a way to avoid what *they do not want*. If your approach to getting to where you want to be is *avoiding* where you do not want to be or whom you do not want to be with, then your dream is not in getting what you want, it's in avoiding what you don't want.

You will never be satisfied or never obtain what you want, even if you have it and are living your dream, because you are operating in an undercurrent of avoidance. This is because you are going to have to stay away from what you don't want, which is why most people never obtain true purpose and joy because they are trying to *avoid* certain issues. They are running away from something instead of toward something.

Some people struggle with a poverty mindset, always avoiding spending money, even if they have it, for fear of losing it. If they are making a sufficient amount of money by living their dream job, ministry, or career, and they have money in the bank as a result, they still avoid poverty because the fear of losing their money haunts them no matter how much or how little money they actually have. Therefore, they are unable to enjoy their dream and the fruits of their labor because they are afraid of losing it. They are running away from poverty instead of toward blessing.

The issue of purpose has nothing to do with getting what you want, but it has everything to do with whether you are running away from something (your cuckoo, your pain, your circumstances) or toward something (passion, joy, your heart's desires, vision).

Many of my clients seek counseling because they are single and desperately want to be married. They are struggling with loneliness, low self-esteem, and past issues of rejection and abandonment. But their desire to be married is more about running away from their pain and loneliness than running toward a healthy, mutually satisfying relationship with another person. Their unresolved pain, fear of being alone, chronic feelings of unworthiness, and fear of rejection will be with them whether they are married or single.

Ask yourself, *Am I using my dream to run away from something or toward something?*

If the answer is yes, what is the pain or issue you are running away from?

_____

_____

_____

_____

_____

We can choose to ignore our pain, but it will manifest itself in other areas of our life, including our dream, and our dream will become a blockage to our purpose. Without purpose and without knowing who we are and what we want, the cuckoos in our life will continuously create issues for us to deal with. Without purpose, the cuckoos become our purpose and lead us to more cuckoos, even cuckoos disguised as our dream.

Finding Purpose Instead of Your Dream

This book is not solely focused on dealing with only one cuckoo from your nest; it is also about creating a long-term, successful strategy to ensure you do not have a nest that is prone to and susceptible to cuckoos. This is what living a life of purpose ensures.

Because breaking free from one cuckoo in your nest might be freeing temporarily, but what happens when (not if) another type of cuckoo tries to enter your nest disguised as something or someone else?

If you have never dealt with the unresolved issues that make your nest vulnerable to cuckoos in the first place, like getting worth and value and identity only from your dream, even good things can become cuckoos.

Finding purpose, as opposed to only your dream, is not just about identifying vision, gifts, strengths, and "what goes right in life." What happens when things go wrong? Purpose comes from our story, not just the good and happy things.

Based on my clinical experience, many people can live to be happy and live their dream. They might have the means, but they lack true meaning. When I work with clients who are wanting to dream big, think positive, and pursue what they love to do, the journey ahead for them cannot ignore their pain, their failures, and their weaknesses. A person's purpose incorporates their story, including their pain, which makes it more meaningful, empowering, and lasting. (The final chapter of this book, "Let Your Eggs Hatch! Treasures from Darkness," shows you how.)

A Story of Pain to Purpose

Emily gracefully pulled me aside after I had just given a presentation at a conference. She said she resonated with what I shared, and she knew she needed to come in for counseling. Emily was carrying a heavy burden. She had been estranged from her parents for years and felt responsible for caring for her mother, who was a stroke victim. As an only child, she faced her mother's financial and health-related decisions alone. Through our sessions together, she realized she was not responsible for her mother's happiness, financial security, and emotional well-being and that her willingness to care, make regular visits, and extend grace was enough. Eventually, she was able to shed the guilt and obligation that had been holding her captive for years.

Emily shared her story of childhood sexual and verbal abuse by her parents. For a very long time she had pushed away the horrific memories of the abuse and wore a mask of happiness so that no one would know the truth about her painful past. She felt ashamed. She had kept her abuse a secret, and even her husband did not know about it until nearly a year into their marriage. In her early forties her anger was roused as the repressed images and memories of her abuse began to emerge. She was no longer able to push down the pain. Emily expressed a desire to work toward healing and forgiveness, but the idea of forgiving her parents was confusing and painful, coupled with struggling to understand why. Emily was a courageous soul with a beautiful testimony of God's healing and grace. She was willing to do the work necessary to receive truth and eventually freedom from her abusive past.

I had the privilege of witnessing her treasure transpire from the darkness of her pain as well as her confidence begin to overshadow her doubts. Our sessions illuminated for her that her words are a gift in her life, because for so long she had been shut down emotionally and verbally, beginning with her childhood abuse and carrying that shame into adulthood. Her voice was stolen and her secret hidden. Emily felt it was a new season for her to embrace her voice and her story as one of power and purpose.

Very shortly after that conversation, she shared with me a realization that her life might have been very different if she had known someone else who had gone through a similar experience. Emily was yearning to share her story of faith and healing as a survivor of abuse and her journey to forgiveness and how counseling changed her life, so she decided to write a book. She was scared and hesitant about the idea, but I could see the joy and excitement behind the veil of her fear. She told me she felt called to share her story so others who were also struggling with hurt, anger, abuse, forgiveness, shame, and self-doubt would discover the hope that she had found. Emily published her book and began speaking publicly. She was passionate about using her voice to give others courage to do the same, so they would no longer suffer silently.

Much to her surprise and delight, more doors opened for her, including radio and television guest appearances as well as winning a book-of-the-year award, which provided even greater opportunities to expand her reach and share her story of freedom.

Emily did not come to counseling with the intention of finding her dream or to be an author or speaker. Through her healing process, she discovered a greater purpose from her pain, and that became a deep-seated joy of her soul. A dream and happiness cannot simply be pursued; they must come from something greater than oneself.

Observation of my clients' purposes post-treatment has revealed that those who allowed purpose and meaning to come from places of pain have significantly less chance of relapsing into their mental illness and corresponding secondary symptoms. Feelings of hopelessness and fears of not being able to cope are significantly reduced. This is because clients are able to move beyond the pain and issues to a permanent place of purpose. This allows each one to operate successfully when life presents future challenges or future cuckoos!

Protect your eggs! Protect your purpose!

Your Purpose Is Bigger than You

I always tell my clients, "If you are terrified and exhilarated at the same time, that's how you know it is God." When you begin your journey into purpose, it will feel scary. And it should feel scary. This feeling is a sign you are on the right path because being afraid is a signal that your purpose is bigger than you are. If you were not passionate about it, there would be no fear associated with it.

There is a distinction between fear of man and fear of God. The fear of God is a reverential fear or awe of his power to move on your behalf in what appear to be impossible situations that are beyond your ability to accomplish. The fear of God is not controlling or evil. You experience the fear of God when you stand back in awe of the goodness he has done as you stand in disbelief, jaw dropped, and think to yourself, *Wow! Look at what God did!*

Purpose has to be big enough that you cannot do it without God. You cannot do it on your own. God deserves the glory because you have a testimony that will be the platform from which others can find encouragement and thus have the faith to pursue their purpose. People of purpose are infectious to be around, and their very presence provides an atmosphere of hope.

Purpose requires faith in God, not faith in self, to accomplish the impossible. Purpose requires a willingness to take a risk and know that God is right there to carry it out.

The [action of His] power that is at work within us, is able to [carry out His purpose and] do superabundantly, far over and above all that we [dare] ask or think [infinitely beyond our highest prayers, desires, thoughts, hopes, or dreams]. (EPH. 3:20 AMPC)

CHAPTER 13

HOW TO LIVE A CUCKOO- FREE LIFE

Embracing Desire, Pursuing Passion, Creating Vision

You must do the things that you think you cannot do.
—ELEANOR ROOSEVELT

THE JOURNEY INTO PURPOSE

The journey to discovering our purpose, our signature eggs, is through embracing the desires of our heart by knowing what we truly want, pursuing our passions, and cocreating a vision for our life with God.

Knowing who we are and what we want means knowing our innermost desires and passions. The more we are connected to the truth of who we are and who God is, the more connected we are to our purpose and therefore, the less prone we are to purpose imposters, allowing cuckoos to invade our lives and become our purpose and ultimately losing ourselves.

The most common phrase clients say when they are engaged in a cuckoo dynamic, whether it is an unhealthy relationship or a self-inflicted behavior, is, "I don't know who I am anymore" or "I've lost myself." This is because their lopsided cuckoo relationships leave them empty, with unmet needs and unfulfilled desires.

People who have a cuckoo in their life have abandoned the journey of discovering their purpose. They have lost hope. Life is hard enough when it comes to following our heart's desires and pursuing our passions. Sadly, hosting the relationship cuckoo or the self-inflicted cuckoo ultimately steals, kills, and destroys our eggs, our purpose, what makes us unique.

When we fail to embrace our desires and passions because we believe they are not possible—or even wrong—we suffer. Yet our passions and desires continually and gently tap at our soul, even though we avoid pursuing them. Suffering occurs when we lose these parts of ourselves, because without our inner compass to guide us, we primarily operate in survival mode in order to cope with our cuckoo's ever-demanding, never-satisfied wants, needs, and desires.

Sacred Desire

Delight yourself also in the LORD, and He shall give you the desires of your heart. (Ps. 37:4)

What if our heart's desires are sacred? What if we revered our heart's desires as holy? What if we saw our heart's desires as from God and for God?

God created us with desires. There are desires within each heart waiting to be discovered and fully embraced. Our true selves, our purpose and reason for being, are to be found in our heart's desires. Desire is at the core of who we are—our hearts. Desire stimulates our search for discovering our purpose and enjoying a meaningful life.

Desires are longings, urges, yearnings, and aches residing in the depths of our heart, our innermost being. Just because you do not experience the desires of your heart does not mean they are not there. I've discovered that people are often unaware of their desires regardless of the fact that our desires are always alive on the inside. In my work, I help my clients to recognize them.

Our heart's desires surprise us in unexpected ways and often go unnoticed or misunderstood. Desires are whispers of our heart subtly trying to get our attention when we least expect it. They sneak up on us through the lyrics of a song, a scene in a movie, the sight of a beautiful flower, through sounds and smells. We often miss our heart's desires because we are looking for them in grander ways, in such milestones as getting married, the birth of a child, being promoted at work, winning an award, or a miracle of some kind. Our desires come in the still, small moments found in the simple pleasures and moments of daily life.

When we neglect or dismiss our heart's desires, we forsake the journey of discovering our purpose. We abandon our eggs. We leave behind the core of who we are and what we want. Instead, we feed the insatiable desires of the cuckoos in our life or we pursue external satisfaction and fulfillment in such things as fame, followers, success, money, promotion, and the approval of others. We strive for perfecting, performing, and producing. We aim to please cuckoos at the cost of losing ourselves.

Delighting yourself in the Lord, embracing your heart's desires, and refusing to allow yourself to delight in your self-inflicted cuckoos or pleasing your cuckoos will be your greatest protection against living a life of unnecessary suffering, ultimately stuck in the Cuckoo Syndrome cycle, which leaves you lost and empty.

What Do You Want?

How do you discover your heart's desires? By knowing what you truly want. As you know, part of the process of dealing with a cuckoo in your life is to set boundaries and use your voice effectively in terms of what you think, what you feel, what you need, and what you want. Wants are about desire, passion, and what brings you joy.

The most significant question I can ask a client is, "What do you want?" Allowing them to identify what they want is about getting them in touch with the desires of their heart and what they are passionate about. Their desires and passions are often dormant, hidden under the toxic weight of the cuckoo in their life.

They have been too busy asking themselves, *What does the cuckoo in my life want?* They are accustomed to thinking about what the cuckoo wants and not what they want.

Many of us grew up in homes or churches believing it was weak, selfish, materialistic, or even sinful to want things, to have desires. We falsely believe we should be satisfied with what we have or else we are ungrateful. We must be content. These unconscious beliefs are limiting, and they block us from the things we want and from the things we enjoy doing. By pursuing our heart's desires, we break these old patterns and heal our wounds.

Jesus is after our hearts. As we saw in chapter 10, "The Religion Cuckoo," Jesus told the religious leaders, the Pharisees and the Sadducees, that their hearts were far from him (Matt. 15:8) because they lived a life governed by rules and by worshiping the law. Jesus awakens desire in us. By pushing away our heart's desires, we are thwarting our innermost being from being alive and receptive to the Spirit's spontaneous voice within us.

Jesus asked, "What do you want Me to do for you?" (Mark 10:51). Pay attention to the question until an answer arises within you. This is how we stay connected to our heart's desires. Pause for a moment. Take a deep breath. What shows up for you right now as you drop into a deep place of desire within your heart? Don't worry about whether it is possible. Don't overthink it. Don't wonder if it's the "right" answer. Don't try to make it appear spiritual, holy, or biblical. Just stay connected to your heart.

Write the answer to Jesus's question here:

_____

_____

_____

Defenses Against Desire

In answering the question "What do you want?" it is normal and expected for many of us to unknowingly use defense mechanisms because defense mechanisms are the lies we tell ourselves to avoid our painful emotions. Getting in touch with what we want and our heart's desires can equate to pain. This is because of its vulnerable nature. Desire begins to feel scary. Longing for something sets us up for rejection, disappointment, and heartache. Because we are afraid of pain, we have a corresponding fear of desire.

We use the following defense mechanisms to dismiss what we really want:

- Minimizing: "It's not that bad." "It could be worse."
- Rationalizing: "I just feel this way because..."
- Denial: "Everything is fine." "I'm OK."
- Intellectualizing: "I can make it better."
- Spiritualizing: "I should just be grateful to God for where I am and stop complaining and wishing things were different."

Which of the defense mechanisms can you most relate to when you answer the question of what you want?

Overcoming Desire Anxiety

Often clients who are engaged in some type of cuckoo dynamic become anxious when they are asked what they want. Many have a hard time sharing the desires of their heart and what they want to do. My goal is to help them to understand that saying what they want triggers anxiety, and then I help them to separate their anxiety from their wants and desires.

Recall from what we said about the anxiety cuckoo in chapter 6 that anxiety can come in the form of what-if statements. When it comes to desires and wants, we often ask, "What if what I want is wrong?" "What if it's not God's plan for my life?" "What if what I want isn't what is best for others, my partner, friends, my church, or my family?" "What if what I want or desire is not God's will?" "What if what I want or desire doesn't happen?" "What if I make a mistake?"

When I see this happening with my clients, I say, "You seem anxious. Do you recognize your feelings of anxiety?" "Notice how you become anxious when you express what you want." It is as if it's wrong or bad for them to say what they want. We process through their anxiety and how they experience it in their thought life and their body. Perhaps they are fidgety, short of breath, have sweaty palms. In this way they learn the connection between sharing with me what they want and how it triggers anxiety.

Together we explore the lies they believe that are associated with what they learned about their wants and the desires of their heart, namely, that these are frivolous, materialistic, selfish, or sinful. We also explore their feelings underneath their desire anxiety, such as fear, shame, and sadness. Once they can put their anxiety aside, they are ready to share and explore what they want and desire and move toward it instead of running away from it.

These questions are related to fear, vulnerability, and lack. How many times in life have we experienced a moment where what we hoped for, wanted, or desired actually happened and then it was suddenly snatched away from us? These past experiences create anxiety and toxic thinking that arise the next time we have a desire or hope for something that we want. We are afraid we will lose what we desire most. As I've said before, anxiety is imagining the future without God in it.

Until we can tolerate risk, vulnerability, and uncertainty, intense feelings of anxiety will destroy the desires of our heart and block us from pursuing what we want to do.

Desire Imposters: Delighting in Idols versus Delighting in the Lord

Recall the scripture, "Delight yourself also in the LORD, and He shall give you the desires of your heart" (Ps. 37:4). From the very beginning, God created us as people of desire. When we encounter pain such as rejection, abandonment, and loss, our hearts become vulnerable, and we are prone to imposter desires that promise to ease our pain.

These imposters take on the form of idols birthed in our hearts and become what we want, because we turn to them every time we are in pain to make us feel better. These idols, even though they are counterfeit desires, become what we desire.

Our answer to the question "What do I want or desire?" becomes about numbing our pain and making ourselves feel better in the moment. Either way these imposter desires drown out our heart's desires. These phony desires do not satisfy the deep longings of our heart.

The desire of a person's heart is uniquely tied to delighting in the Lord. But when we delight in our idols, our self-inflicted cuckoos, or our cuckoo-coping companions, they create the notion that our desires are evil and wrong. Therefore, we subconsciously attach shame to our desires and passions. Idols and cuckoo-coping companions include food, sex, work, television, social media, alcohol, drugs, sleep, busyness, other people, and even our ministry. Operating from a place of shame disconnects us from God, our heart's true desires, and eventually from our purpose.

Thus, unhealthy or addictive behaviors can manifest as misplaced desires because we are placing our desires in our idols. When our God-given desires are misplaced, they lead to more pain and suffering.

When we make the choice to ask for help and embrace the healing process, we can turn away from delighting in our idols to delighting in God. Therefore, our God-given desires emerge from a healthy place, which brings freedom from suffering and reconnects us to God and our purpose.

Holy Frustration

Often we feel guilty when we are frustrated or discontented with our life or our relationships. "Why can't I just learn to be happier in my marriage, work, ministry, church, community, group of friends?" We believe everyone else is content with their life and doing just fine, so we feel guilty, selfish about our chronic disappointment and lack of fulfillment.

One of the indicators we have a cuckoo in our life is that, deep down, we feel like something is off, something is missing. But we cannot put our finger on how or why. We just know we are suffering. In the quiet moments of the day, we feel a plaguing sensation, an emptiness, a yearning for something else. We falsely believe something must be wrong, not with our circumstances or relationships but with us.

It is important to refuse to accept the fact that this is the way things are or must be or always will be. Cuckoo relationships become familiar; we get used to them. They are invisible enemies. We gradually become deceived, and our own heart's desires are snuffed out. This is just the way things are, we tell ourselves. We become stuck and trapped. The truth is that we are experiencing a holy frustration. We are frustrated and discontented because something is wrong, not because we are wrong.

We tend to hide our desires and keep them a secret from God and even ourselves because we feel ashamed. What we do not realize is that our frustrations can be a signal to us that God is trying to get our attention to move us out of our current season of suffering into a new season of blessing and heart's desires. But we must be honest with what we really want to do.

There are difficult seasons we must go through that are necessary for the desires of our heart to be fulfilled. Often our desires will get us into seasons where we say, "I didn't expect for this to happen! In fact, it feels worse than it did before." You might have received a promise or a vision from God and became so excited, and then everything that could go wrong did. This is part of the process.

Our frustrations will save us from handing over our purpose in life to cuckoos and sacrificing our heart's desires of "I'll just stay as I am." This lifestyle will never fully satisfy you. Compromising your eggs, your purpose, is not worth suffering the slow death of a thousand cuts for someone or something that doesn't belong in your nest, in your life, in the first place.

Moving in Faith Instead of Fear

Now that we have discovered the what—*what* you want and *what* your heart's desires are—let's address *how* to pursue them. The how requires movement and action on our part to take steps in the direction of pursuing what we want and our heart's desires. Many people take a passive approach rather than an active approach because they are afraid. Either they experience desire anxiety or they are afraid what they want is not what God wants. The result is the same. They stand still in fear instead of taking steps in faith.

The only way to know if your heart's desires will come to pass is to go after them. Sometimes we are waiting for God to give us a sign, and we pray, *God if this is your will, show me.* We are waiting for him to do certain things, and he is waiting for us to move. By pursuing your heart's desires, you are saying, *God, I trust you and your grace. If I make a misstep, you grace will cover me, and I trust you to show me if I need to change direction.*

We believe we are in faith when we are still and pray for God's will about our heart's desires and ask him to tell us what we should want, but we are actually in fear. This is because we are afraid we are going to miss his will or make a mistake or be disappointed. It takes faith to move forward and pursue true desires and wants.

God not only wants you to trust him when you do not know the answer, he also wants you to trust yourself, to trust your own heart.

God is interested in giving you the desires of your heart. You will go about bringing into existence and confirming that your desires are from God because you will begin to see them come to pass in your daily life. Jesus asked, "What do you want Me to do for you?" (Mark 10:51).

In regard to pursuing your heart's desires, this is what you don't want to do:

> Fear = Doing nothing while continuing to pray and ask God what his will is and what he wants, waiting rather than moving, and falsely believing you are "in faith."

This is what you want to do:

> Faith = Taking action, pursuing the desires of your heart,
> and taking steps to do what you want to do.

Approach your desires with an open mindset, letting go of expectations and leaning on your own understanding. The outcome might look different but still satisfy the deep longings of your heart. As you step out in faith, you are not only overcoming your fear but also allowing God to open and close the doors along the way. He will protect you and guide you. Let your wants and desires unfold as you go along. But you must do something to move in the direction of your desires.

Don't run from desire; embrace it and run toward it.

Passion: The Key to Purpose

Once you discover what you want and begin to take the steps of faith to pursue your heart's desires, you can identify what you are passionate about. Passion is a specific outward sign, a clue, an indication of what you want, a manifestation of your inner desires. Passion is an external way to pursue your heart's desires and move you closer to discovering your purpose and living a cuckoo-free life.

Paskho is the ancient Greek word for "passion." This equates to the passion Jesus had for us that manifested in his crucifixion, his pain because of his deep love for us. There is a connection between pain and passion that gives meaning to suffering. Passion is an intense emotion, a compelling feeling, an enthusiasm, or a desire for something. Passion overcomes pain, resistance, opposition, criticism, and all other obstacles.

Finding passion means we have found our place of purpose. Many people experience difficulty knowing what their passion is because of the suffering in their life. Their purpose has been smothered by their cuckoos for so long that they lose their passion. I use the following questions with my clients to assist them in beginning the process of rediscovering their purpose and identifying their passion:

- What is the deepest desire of my heart?
- When I read or search the web, what material am I most drawn to?
- What do I want to do with my life?
- What would bring me the utmost fulfillment?
- What are my unique gifts, talents, and strengths?
- Where would I love to live?
- What do I love to do so much that I forget to sleep or eat?
- What is the idea that never leaves my mind?
- What do I continually imagine about my future?
- What is the most important thing I want to do in my life?
- What do I feel truly excited about?
- What are my reoccurring dreams?
- What am I inspired to do?

- What would I want to do more than anything else, even if I was never paid for it?
- Who inspires me most?
- What makes me come alive?

Imagination: The Vehicle for Vision and the Foundation for Purpose

Imagination is cocreating our future purpose with Jesus and encompasses envisioning our heart's desires and seeing our passions come to life. Imagination is the template for our vision. Imagination is an essential tool in connecting us with the Holy Spirit and the unseen realm because it is designed by God as a template to sense his presence and hear his voice speaking within us.

The word *imagination* means "the act or power of forming a mental image of something not present to the senses."[25] Imagination requires a picture or image and also means to conceive of or to form a purpose. The definition of imagination reveals similarities to how faith is described in Scripture:

Faith is the assurance (the confirmation, the title deed) of the things [we] hope for, being the proof of things [we] do not see and the conviction of their reality [faith perceiving as real fact what is not revealed to the senses]. (HEB. 11:1 AMPC)

Using our imagination requires faith to envision the things we hope for as a reality even though they are not yet seen and have not yet happened.

We often think of imagination as unrealistic, unimportant, childish, impractical, and not sensible to real-life matters. Imagination is a function of the right brain and includes characteristics such as flexibility, artistry, fantasy, visualization, intuition, empathy, and sensitivity.

Additionally, we can change our brains simply by imagining. From a neuroscientific point of view, imagining an act and doing it are not so different.

> Brain scans show that in action and imagination many of the same parts of the brain are activated. For example, when people close their eyes to visualize the letter a, the primary visual cortex lights up just as it would if they were actually looking at the letter a. Imagining an act engages the same motor and sensory programs that are involved in doing it.[26]

The more you take the time to imagine what your heart desires and what you want, the closer you are to allowing it to become a reality in your life.

Vision: Cocreating Our Purpose with God

> Where there is no vision . . . the people perish.
> (Prov. 29:18 AMPC)

Imagine for a moment the reed warbler in the illustration in chapter 1 feeding the grotesque-looking cuckoo chick. Prior to the cuckoo landing in her nest, she was sitting on her own eggs and envisioning them hatching, feeding her young, caring for them, and experiencing a deep sense of pride and purpose in what she had created and birthed.

Then, suddenly, her vision is ripped away from her when the cuckoo chick is dropped in her nest and hatches first, destroying the reed warbler's eggs. All she sees now is her cuckoo chick. Her vision has been obstructed by the cuckoo. Her own eggs have perished.

Establishing a vision and protecting it from unhealthy relationships and self-sabotaging behaviors is your guide to living a cuckoo-free life.

Having a Vision = Seeing Your Eggs Hatch and Come to Life

Vision is the foundation that allows your passions and heart's desires to manifest. Vision is an essential component to create, nurture, and deliver your purpose. Vision is a promise from God and the vehicle for which we cocreate our purpose with him, using our heart's desires, passions, and imagination.

Now that you have awakened what you want and embraced your heart's desires, the next step in discovering your purpose is establishing your vision. This process entails adjusting your mind to expect and receive a vision. Vision encompasses your entire being spiritually, relationally, and emotionally. Vision is the key to unlock the future doors of purpose in your life and requires faith in God. Remember, purpose is always bigger than you.

The Key to Vision Is Writing It Down

I tell my clients that the hand will write what the mouth cannot speak.

> *I will [in my thinking] stand upon my post of observation and station myself on the tower or fortress, and will watch to see what He will say within me and what answer I will make [as His mouthpiece]....*

> *And the Lord answered me and said, Write the vision and engrave it so plainly upon tablets that everyone who passes may [be able to] read [it easily and quickly] as he hastens by.*

*For the vision is yet for an appointed time and it hastens to the
end [fulfillment]; it will not deceive or disappoint. Though it
tarry, wait [earnestly] for it, because it will surely come; it will
not be behindhand on its appointed day.* (HAB. 2:1–3 AMPC,
emphasis added)

Gathering wisdom from this passage, I developed the
following principles for writing out your vision:

- Observe and watch to see what God will say within us,
  emphasizing he speaks to us.
- What answer we will make as his mouthpiece; we have the
  answer within us.
- The Lord's answer is to write the vision and engrave it on
  tablets (a journal, a notebook, or a computer).
- The vision is for an appointed time and will reach its fulfillment; it will not deceive or disappoint. Have faith and be
  expectant!
- Wait earnestly for it, because it will surely come; it will not
  be delayed on its appointed day. Be patient, trust God's
  timing, and don't give up or lose heart.

Too Good to Be True

After many months of contemplation, discontent, and confusion, I followed the above steps when I was writing out my
own vision that led me to start my practice. During that time
it seemed like an impossible, daunting task, coupled with fear
and many roadblocks. I still recall the afternoon I was sitting
on the sofa in my office with so many voices and opinions of
others swirling around in my head on what decision I should
make. After stilling my heart and thoughts, I asked myself,
"What would I want God to say to me? What do I really want?"

That was my way of putting my own thoughts and fears aside so I could hear from him.

The primary ways most people communicate with God is through journaling and prayer. Although these are powerful and effective, they are also a one-way conversation of us pouring our thoughts, desires, requests, and feelings before God. Asking the above questions and writing down your corresponding vision allows for a dialogue with God so you can experience him speaking back to you.

For me, God continued to repeat the phrase "too good to be true" from my vision often throughout my life because that is his way of showing me it *is* him in the midst of seemingly impossible situations. I tend to be perfectionistic and get stuck in my own head, so I ask myself, "What would seem too good to be true?" It releases my imagination and the Holy Spirit to minister to my heart.

I have taken countless clients through this same vision exercise, and they have found the faith needed to pursue their purpose based on their heart's desires and passions. First, I give them a blank piece of paper with a clipboard and tell them to get cozy. I tell them to close their eyes and imagine that Jesus has walked into the room and is sitting beside them. Then I say, "What would you want Jesus to say to you? Not what do you think he would say. Not what do you think is his will. Instead, what would seem too good to be true? Now start writing it down in the first person as if he were speaking directly to you and answering the question. You are his mouthpiece."

They look at me as if I were crazy, but after they finish, I read it back to them, with their eyes closed. They always respond in tears, "I did not write that!" or "That does not sound like me." Then I read them Habakkuk 2:1–3 to reinforce their faith in God's Word. This helps them get out of their left-brain thinking into their right brain, creating and feeling so their imagination would be open to the Holy Spirit.

Some of my clients feel immediately assured and confident that their vision is from God, and some have a difficult time receiving it and believing it. This is normal. It's about being vulnerable. How can it not be? They just named their real desire for the first time! It is only after they have had some time to meditate on it that they come to wholeheartedly embrace it and eventually step out in faith and start pursuing it.

This is a step-by-step process, and the adventure is in walking through the doors that only God can open. Let us not underestimate the power of the Holy Spirit, who is actively at work behind the scenes on behalf of our vision! Vision begins as a dream and carries with it the idea that it is too big, too impossible to bring into the reality of everyday life.

It has been awe-inspiring to be a part of the journey when a client's vision manifests and reaches its fulfillment. Essentially, I'm witnessing their eggs hatch and come to life, no longer destroyed by their cuckoos.

This is the foundational pathway to discovering your purpose and allowing your eggs to hatch so you can live a cuckoo-free life:

Purpose = Your Dream + Your Vision + Your Passion + Your Heart's Desires
+ God's Calling on Your Life + Your Story + Your Pain

A Time to Write

I encourage you to write your vision for your purpose. Go to a quiet, private place by yourself for a while. Your favorite spot to just be, void of distraction. Bring a blank notebook or journal along. Take a deep breath and let your imagination flow. Focus on what you want, your passions, and your heart's deepest desires. Envision them coming to life. Invite Jesus into the space with you.

See him asking you, "What do you want me to do for you?" Put aside your desire anxieties and your fears of what seems impossible and stop overthinking. Don't get stuck wondering how to write this correctly. Write in the first person what you would want Jesus to say to you that would seem too good to be true.

You'll be surprised what is waiting in your heart.

CHAPTER 14

LET YOUR EGGS HATCH!

Treasures from Darkness

The greater the difficulty, the more the glory in surmounting it.
—Epictetus

And I will give you treasures hidden in the darkness—secret riches. (Isa. 45:3 NLT)

EVERY PERSON HAS A TREASURE. JUST AS WE *ALL* HAVE A cuckoo.

Purpose, like treasure, often comes from darkness and hidden places.

Part of your story and what makes you unique is the process of uncovering the treasure hidden in the dirt of your life and exposing it in all its beauty.

If we are not in touch with the darkness of the pain from the cuckoos in our life, we cannot discover the purpose (or treasure) the darkness contains. We're talking about, essentially, your eggs! Your treasure and your purpose are the neglected eggs in your nest that have been smothered by the cuckoo.

The Courageous Step of Finding Your Treasure

Olivia was experiencing severe emotional ups and downs every day and was having trouble managing the stress of her demanding job. Initially, we focused on treating her depression and discovered her intense need to fix herself, which was keeping her in a place of perfectionism and self-hatred, and she believed her pain was somehow her fault. I helped her to understand that she was not a project but a person who deserved self-compassion rather than harsh judgment. I would often redirect her why questions ("Why do I do this?") to what ("What am I feeling?") in order to connect her with her heart's desires and emotions. She was accustomed to dismissing her emotions and disconnecting from her needs because of her high need to know at the cost of truly knowing herself, which was deeply rooted in shame.

Olivia grew up in a home where she learned from her father that women should not have a voice because their opinions were not important and their beliefs were never correct. Being raised in an emotionally abusive home fueled her distrust of her own heart, emotions, and decisions. Once she was able to heal from these wounds, through our work together, she discovered one of the reasons she was experiencing so much suffering and frustration around her day-to-day activities at work. She was undergoing a great deal of dissatisfaction with her job.

She felt angry, sad, and afraid all within the course of a typical workday, but she was ashamed that she experienced those feelings about a role that looked like anyone else's dream job. Instead of allowing herself to feel and express her feelings in an effort to change the situation, she turned her feelings into weapons and attacked herself for what she felt and thought, and therefore she felt stuck.

While focusing on her treasure throughout our sessions, I observed a pattern. Olivia would avidly take notes and ask many questions, no longer from a place of why or to fix herself but out of a genuine aspiration for personal growth and healing. I noticed her passion and curiosity for the counseling process. She also spent much of her free time reading blogs and books on the subject of helping people and understanding human behavior.

I paid attention to this and slowly began to speak to this treasure in her and draw it out from the hidden places of her pain. I could clearly see that her shame and suffering related to trying to fix herself were a misplaced passion and a distortion of her purpose and desire to help others. Her struggles in this particular area were a misrepresentation of her place of strength, which was actually empowering for her instead of painful.

Through exploring her discontentment and frustration with her job—giving her permission to be honest with what she *really* wanted and what kind of work was better suited to her values— she discovered for herself that she was passionate about helping people and had a gift for mentoring others through their career struggles, a talent that had already earned her a positive reputation within her organization.

She embraced her passion and took the courageous step of beginning a side business as a career coach to find ways to grow that gift into a new career as well as embrace her purpose. As of today, Olivia has left her corporate job and has grown her coaching business to full time.

Your Signature Struggles Become Your Signature Strengths

A person's greatest place of pain is their greatest place of power, and their area of weakness is their area of gifting.

Typically, clients do not come into counseling and say, "I don't have a purpose and that is my problem." Essentially they are suffering from the cuckoos in their life. Clients seek treatment for a *presenting problem*, which is just a fancy clinical term for issues and challenges that are present in their life, places of pain and weakness they develop to cope with their pain.

The majority of my clients do not say, "I don't have a purpose and that is my issue." They seek treatment for their cuckoo dynamic, a presenting problem that is causing suffering: depression, anxiety, broken relationships, unexplained medical symptoms, trauma, addiction, and so forth. I am the one who is aware that their pain (darkness) holds the key to unlocking their purpose (treasure). This is because purpose, like treasure, is often hidden underneath the darkness of the cuckoo's toxicity.

The purpose (the eggs in your nest) that your cuckoo is smothering and destroying, as well as the corresponding pain that it creates, is the exact place where your purpose, gifting, and power resides. My clients not only learn how to heal from their presenting problem and break free of allowing cuckoos in their nest, but they create a space to nurture and care for their eggs in order for them to hatch and come to life. Their areas of pain and weakness provide clues to their gifts and purpose.

A Story of Pain to Purpose

When Vivien came in for her first session, she was a closed book. She did not want to be in counseling *again*, but she was strongly encouraged to do so by a close and supportive family member. She was recently diagnosed with clinical depression and had been in and out of counseling, including several intensive outpatient programs, but to no avail. I asked her questions to engage and received no response. The sixty-minute session was held in complete silence. In fact, she would not even make eye contact with me.

Due to knowing her mental health, family background, and psychiatric history, I had a notion she was repeating a false narrative based on earlier wounds and wanted me to fire her as a client. I thought perhaps she subconsciously was trying to prove to herself that she was not worth fighting for. She was familiar with the pain of abandonment, which stemmed from her relationship with her father. But I was not going to give up on her, even though the following sessions were the same: silent hours.

As I continued to sit across from her, I began to look for her treasure. My heart ached for Vivien as I could see lines upon lines of scars where she had cut herself. I noticed her tattoos, jewelry, and clothing choices revealed a theme of music and animals, clues to her passions. I said, "I see you like music. Do you play any instruments?" She looked at me for the first time and hesitantly mumbled a yes. I invited her to bring her guitar to our next session and play whatever she wanted. When she played, she began to communicate with me, and the ice around her heart began to thaw.

In the months that followed she shared her heartache and her pain, and healing gradually began to occur. She stopped cutting herself and eventually became sober. I also learned more about her treasure. She had a deep love for animals, and the way she described her house was as if it were a zoo because of the multitude of pets she adopted. Vivien explained that she had dreamed of being a veterinarian since she was a girl, so I asked her what it would look like if she pursued her passion for animals. She began by volunteering at a veterinary clinic, which turned into a job opportunity, and she also began playing her guitar and singing around town. Vivien graduated from counseling soon after.

There was a particular session she recalls to this day when we discussed how veterinary medicine was her passion. My hope was to plant a seed in her heart by helping her envision that perhaps she would one day talk about her life in veterinary school. She said she brushed it off at the time because of her doubts, fears, and feelings of inadequacy.

A few years later I received a phone call from her to resume counseling because her significant other, Kevin, had committed suicide. She coped with the pain around this trauma by relapsing into addictive behaviors. In her sessions, Vivien processed her unresolved grief and previously avoided painful emotions and identified the lies she had been telling herself surrounding the traumatic loss she experienced. During this season of counseling, she told me that she desired to explore her faith at a deeper level. She mentioned how grateful she was for the way I had treated her relationship with God as any other important person in her life, and she often felt as if he was sitting on the sofa beside her. She mentioned that I unknowingly modeled for her the unconditional love of God, who did not abandon her during difficult times but was there to help her.

She became a sponsor for a twelve-step program and greatly enjoyed being a mentor and confidant to others on their journey to sobriety. They were deeply encouraged by her story of healing, which she would often share at meetings. What she enjoyed most was having the opportunity to sit with people in the same pain and shame that she had felt and being able to offer hope.

Vivien started to rebuild her life by reigniting her childhood passion and taking the necessary educational steps to pursue a career in veterinary medicine, which continued to be a hidden desire of her heart. Many times she suffered with feelings of inadequacy, believing it was too late for her because she was older than most of the students applying to veterinary school, and statistics showed there was a less than 10 percent acceptance rate. But she decided to overcome her fear of failure and rejection and applied to several universities.

I received a phone call from her a few months later, and she shared the good news that she had been accepted at her top-choice university. She said it seemed too good to be true, but she knew it was of God. She remembered the seed that was planted in her heart during one of our sessions all those years ago, during her darkest time, and she couldn't wait to sit on my sofa just as we had envisioned and tell me about her life in veterinary school. And she did.

The Enemy of Purpose

He was a murderer from the beginning, and does not stand in the truth because there is no truth in him. When he lies, he speaks what is natural to him, for he is a liar and the father of lies and half-truths. (John 8:44 AMP)

There is indeed another key player who is invested in ensuring our pain remains unresolved and our purpose destroyed. This enemy is the serpent cuckoo, Satan, the Father of Lies.

Satan's role is to thwart our God-given purpose. Satan knows which cuckoos to deceptively send to our nest. This is because Satan knows that when we live from our purpose, we have a powerful testimony through which we expand God's kingdom here on earth by bringing freedom and healing to others. Additionally, our purpose is the place where we experience a deep-seated joy and intimacy in Christ.

For those reasons, Satan will do everything in his power to ensure we endure suffering and experience pain and weakness in those *exact* places of our passions, gifting, and purpose, and he does this through the specific lies he tries to reinforce throughout our life.

Satan seeks to twist every painful encounter with a family member, romantic partner, colleague, or friend to strengthen the original lie stemming from our first encounter with a painful experience in childhood. This is because the lies are familiar. They feel true, so we have a tendency to believe them. For example, as a child, your best friend stopped spending time with you and chose to be with another more popular friend instead. You felt rejected and believed you were not good enough. As an adult, when your close friend does not have as much time to spend with you, you feel rejected and believe you must have done something wrong to lose the friendship. In reality, that is not true; your friend is just unusually busy. Satan wants you to falsely believe there is a pattern in your life of rejections from multiple friends, but the truth is that there are life circumstances that bring unexpected changes to those relationships, and none of them are your fault or a result of you not being good enough, pretty enough, smart enough, or popular enough. Those are all lies rooted in painful encounters that seek to destroy the joy and security of your friendships today.

The greatest treasures are often buried in the deepest, darkest places. Therefore, there is a connection between treasure and darkness, pain and power, gifting and weakness, which is directly tied to purpose, as it gives meaning to suffering. Many people cannot see their treasure beyond their cuckoos and the pain they inflict. That is where my own purpose as a counselor comes in as one who has the insight to draw out the treasure.

It is important to look for these signs when working with clients by finding clues in their presenting problem and where they struggle. Where is their purpose misplaced? What desires and passions are they ashamed of? Where have their passions become painful? What specific lies do they believe? I ask these questions for this reason:

Their places of pain, suffering, and weakness point me toward their passion, gifting, and power, which will eventually become the platform for their God-given purpose and destiny.

For example, Ben was constantly criticized as a young boy by his father for never being good enough, no matter how hard he tried. He was continually told that he was stupid, wimpy, and weak. He loved taking photos, but his father accused him of being feminine and told him photography was a waste of time.

When Ben became an adolescent, other painful experiences built on the lies his father told him and reinforced them in his own heart. Ben was rejected by his girlfriend, who said he was too wimpy. His football coach consistently put him on the bench no matter how hard he practiced. His teacher was unaware of his dyslexia and accused him of being lazy, unproductive, and unintelligent.

As an adult, Ben's wife complained about him not being home enough and not spending enough time with her and the children due to his demanding workload. And then he was fired from his job because of budget cuts. He gradually began having one too many drinks at night to cope with his feelings of failure and inadequacy and frequently viewing pornography when he could not sleep due to his intense anxiety. All of this only contributed to the shame he already felt. He suffered with insomnia, was diagnosed with depression and anxiety, and eventually separated from his family because he was ashamed and believed they deserved better.

After working through his pain in counseling, Ben disclosed he never liked sports and only played football to please his father to prove he was not feminine. He regretted not pursuing art and photography in college and graduated with an engineering degree instead. His true passion and gifting was expressed artistically.

One of the many reasons Ben fell in love with his wife was because she was the first person to tell him he was strong, and she greatly enjoyed his photography. He felt tremendously sad and guilty that he wasn't home enough to spend time with her and his children because he worked long hours at his engineering firm to please his boss and prove to his family he was successful and intelligent. What he really wanted was to be home for dinner every night, take photos to feed his soul, and tuck his children into bed while hearing all about their day.

Through his journey of healing, Ben eventually went off his depression and anxiety medication, stopped using alcohol and pornography to medicate his pain, and overcame the lie that he was not good enough, weak, and stupid. He began marital counseling with his wife to restore their relationship, and he took photography classes at a local university. His greatest joy was spending time every night with his boys.

Ben started a website to post his photos, and his pastor noticed it and asked him if he would be willing to take photos for the church. It was the first time he felt validated by a father figure in an area he was passionate about, and it gave him the courage to let his creative, artistic side out and not hide his true self.

At his new job, many opportunities arose for Ben to start conversations with other men who were struggling in their marriages, burned out and overworked, having affairs, drinking too much, watching too much pornography, and experiencing depression with no sign of hope. Eventually, they started meeting monthly, and their men's group grew to hundreds of people, as men brought their friends and word spread like wildfire around their community. Ben's greatest places of pain and his areas of weakness became a place of power, gifting, and purpose.

Taking Back Your Purpose

The greatest cuckoo of all is the lies we believe about ourselves, an invisible enemy disguising itself as truth and telling us that the areas that cause us the most pain are exactly the places we should avoid.

The truth is this: what begins as a painful encounter eventually becomes a valuable treasure.

Looking back over my own life, I can honestly say the greatest treasures have been discovered during the darkest times of my life. Over the years, weaknesses have given way to strengths, failures have led to successes, pain has led to power and passion, grief has manifested in joy, and God has used it all for his glory and his purpose.

Perhaps you have allowed a few too many cuckoos in your life. Perhaps you have some missing, cracked, or crushed eggs that have never hatched. Perhaps your story is not anywhere near what you hoped or expected it would be. One thing is for certain: it is never too late to begin again.

You can discover your treasure in the darkest of places. You can get back what the cuckoo has taken. And you can find the purpose you've never been able to live.

To work with Andrea directly or to schedule an appointment, please visit her website at www.andreaandersonpolk.com.

ACKNOWLEDGMENTS

To my publisher, Jonathan Merkh, you went above and beyond. Thank you for believing in me, catching the vision, and sharing my passion for those who are suffering. You are more than a marvelous publisher. You are a friend and a man of wisdom and compassion.

To the wonderful team at Forefront Books, your gracious leadership allowed this book to become a reality. A sincere "thank you" for your patience, enthusiasm, and expertise in coming alongside me to get this book into the hands of many others. Special thanks to Justin Batt, Lauren Ward, and Jennifer Gingerich. You three are sensational and I'm endlessly grateful. Thank you to illustrator and interior designer Bill Kersey for making the cuckoo jump off the page and into hearts. And to designer Bruce Gore for the beautiful cover.

To John Sloan, my editor extraordinaire, I appreciate your dedication, expert feedback, and thoughtful care of me and my work. Thank you from the bottom of my heart for your instrumental contribution in bringing this book to fruition.

To John Scanlon, thank you for your outstanding counsel as an attorney and friend. You kept me between the guardrails and encouraged me along the way.

Thank you to my marketing team, Steve and Jason, and the folks at The Dobbins Group. Special thanks to the incredible executive coaching I received from Pepper Bullock and Joseph Bowers of Safe Harbor Consulting and to Keri Childers of Keri Childers

Consulting for her unrelenting passion, ambition, and guidance. Ash Greyson, I appreciate you being a levelheaded, thoughtful, and caring voice.

My deepest gratitude to my clients, the men and women who have courageously shared their stories of healing, transformation, and hope. Each one of you is an inspiration, and I am honored to be called your counselor. You are the heart and soul of this book.

A heartfelt thank-you to my family. Words cannot adequately acknowledge the influence of the person who taught me the true meaning of unconditional love, my mother. The influence of your ever-present care is the light that shines through this book and that formed who I am.

To my brother and sisters, you are not just siblings, but my closest friends. David, your ability to hit the bulls-eye of my heart carries me through the good and bad. Thank you for being a big reality check and my cheerleader who makes me laugh when I want to cry and cry when I want to laugh. To Ashley, your intuition and spiritual discernment have served as a constant reminder of God's heart toward me throughout my life. To Liz, "Bubby," you went from being my baby sister to my favorite person on the planet. To my brothers-in-law, Brandon and Brad, you have such tender souls; thank you for loving me like a sister.

My heart-bursting amount of love to Uncle Bobby. I love you with my whole heart.

In loving memory of my grandmother, Ga-Ga. I only wish you were still here so I could personally thank you. You showed me what safe feels like. Your love is far-reaching and everlasting. You are the very best of everything.

To Peter and Pam, thank you for loving me like a daughter. What a precious gift to have parents-in-law who are so loving, supportive, and giving of themselves.

To my dear friend Michelle Mays, thank you for your wise yet witty counsel and for giving generously of your time at the shortest notice. I am deeply grateful for your emotional support and loving friendship that has nourished my soul through the years. Your insight is invaluable. To Cyndi Wagner, thank you for being a steadfast friend from our time together in graduate school to this day and beyond.

A very special thank you to my phenomenal pastors and mentors, Pastor Barry, Pastor Bill, Pastor Joan, Sally, and Terry, to whom I owe so much of my own spiritual journey. Each of you taught me so much about wholeness and guided me toward intimacy with Jesus as I was becoming a young woman.

Finally, to my husband, Dan, all the words in the world couldn't express the magnitude of my appreciation. You know me better than I know myself. Thank you for showing me that true love isn't just a fairy tale. And thank you for sneaking into my office so many times to remind me that it was time to have fun and rest. I love to write, but I love you more. Let's go be big kids. Thank you for a life filled with adventure. You are wild and wonderful.

To my readers, blessings to each of you as you journey toward healing and wholeness. You are all precious treasures. May you live a life free of cuckoos and full of purpose.

NOTES

Chapter 1: The Cuckoo in Your Nest: Do Your Relationships Resemble Cuckoos?

1 Oldřich Mikulica, *The Cuckoo: The Uninvited Guest* (Plymouth, UK: Wild Nature Press, 2016), 16.

2 "Parasite," *The American Heritage Dictionary of the English Language* (New York: HarperCollins, 2022).

3 Jesse Greenspan, "The Brilliant Ways Parasitic Birds Terrorize Their Victims," *Audubon,* February 25, 2016, https://www.audubon.org/news/the-brilliant-ways-parasitic-birds-terrorize-their-victims.

4 Wikipedia, s.v. "Cuckoo," accessed December 5, 2015, https://en.wikipedia.org/w/index.php?title=Cuckoo&oldid=692439720

5 Wikipedia, s.v. "Cuckoo."

6 Greenspan, "The Brilliant Ways Parasitic Birds Terrorize Their Victims."

7 Greenspan, "The Brilliant Ways Parasitic Birds Terrorize Their Victims."

8 Mikulica, *The Cuckoo,* 7.

9 Nick Davies, *Cuckoo: Cheating by Nature* (New York: Bloomsbury USA, 2015), 184.

10 William Feeney, "Egg colours make cuckoos masters of disguise," *The Conversation,* November 19, 2014, https://theconversation.com/egg-colours-make-cuckoos-masters-of-disguise-34217.

Chapter 2: Stuck in Cuckoo Land: How to Deal with the Cuckoos in Your Life

11 Ian Tucker, "Claire Spottiswoode: Host and parasite birds are competing in a great egg race," *The Guardian,* June 3, 2011, https://www.theguardian.com/environment/2011/jun/05/claire-spottiswoode-evolution-birds-eggs.

12 Ian Tucker, "Claire Spottiswoode."

Chapter 3: The Cuckoo of Not Feeling Your Feelings: What Happens When You Avoid Emotions?

13 Jack W. Hayford et al., eds., *New Spirit Filled Life Bible* (Nashville: Thomas Nelson, 2002), 1317.

14 "Epipotheo," BibleTools, https://www.bibletools.org/index.cfm/fuseaction/Lexicon.show/ID/G1971/epipotheo.htm.

15 Hayford, *New Spirit Filled Life Bible,* 1638.

Chapter 5: What Feeds a Cuckoo?: Lies We Believe and Defenses We Use

16 Merriam-Webster's Online Dictionary, s.v. "reality," accessed April 8, 2017, http://www.merriam-webster.com/dictionary/reality.

17 "Aletheia," https://www.bibletools.org/index.cfm/fuseaction/Lexicon.show/ID/G225/aletheia.htm.

18 "Ginosko," Bible Hub, https://biblehub.com/greek/1097.htm.

Chapter 6: The Fear Cuckoo: A Subtle Cuckoo in Disguise

19 C. S. Lewis, *A Grief Observed* (New York: HarperCollins Publishers), p. 69.

20 Jack W. Hayford et al., eds., *New Spirit Filled Life Bible* (Nashville: Thomas Nelson, 2002), 1837.

21 Bill Gaultiere, "'Fear Not!' 365 Days a Year," SoulShepherding, n.d., https://www.soulshepherding.org/fear-not-365-days-a-year/.

Chapter 12: The Antidote to Cuckoos: Discovering Your Purpose

22 Jesse Greenspan, "The Brilliant Ways Parasitic Birds Terrorize Their Victims," *Audubon,* February 25, 2016, https://www.audubon.org/news/the-brilliant-ways-parasitic-birds-terrorize-their-victims.

23 Ian Tucker, "Claire Spottiswoode: Host and parasite birds are competing in a great egg race," *The Guardian,* June 3, 2011, https://www.theguardian.com/environment/2011/jun/05/claire-spottiswoode-evolution-birds-eggs.

24 Tucker, "Claire Spottiswoode."

Chapter 13: How to Live a Cuckoo-Free Life: Embracing Desire, Pursuing Passion, Creating Vision

25 Merriam-Webster's Online Dictionary, s.v. "imagination," accessed April 8, 2017, http://www.merriam-webster.com/dictionary/imagination.

26 Norman Doidge, *The Brain That Changes Itself: Stories of Personal Triumph from the Frontiers of Brain Science* (New York: Penguin, 2007), 203–204.